BASEBALL

★ ★ ★ YESTERDAY & TODAY ★ ★ ★

BASEBALL
Yesterday & Today

Josh Leventhal

Voyageur Press

First published in 2006 by Voyageur Press, an imprint of MBI Publishing Company, Galtier Plaza, Suite 200, 380 Jackson Street, St. Paul, MN 55101-3885 USA

MBI Publishing Company titles are also available at discounts in bulk quantity for industrial or sales-promotional use. For details write to Special Sales Manager at MBI Publishing Company, Galtier Plaza, Suite 200, 380 Jackson Street, St. Paul, MN 55101-3885 USA

Library of Congress Cataloging-in-Publication Data

Leventhal, Josh, 1971-
  Baseball yesterday & today / Josh Leventhal.
    p. cm.
  Includes index.
  ISBN-13: 978-0-7603-2646-6 (plc w/ jacket)
  ISBN-10: 0-7603-2646-0 (plc w/ jacket)
  1. Baseball--United States--History. I. Title.
  GV863.A1L48 2006
  796.357--dc22

                              2006016661

Editor: Josh Leventhal
Designer: Julie Vermeer

Printed in China

On the front cover: Joe Jackson, circa 1918.
On the back cover: (top) West Side Grounds, Chicago, 1908, and Chase Field, Phoenix, 1998. (bottom) George Gibson, Pittsburgh Pirates, circa 1908, and Bengie Molina, Toronto Blue Jays, 2006.
On the title page: (left) Otis Clymer, Washington Senators, and Red Kleinow, New York Yankees, Hilltop Park, New York, 1909. (right) Vladimir Guerrero, Los Angeles Angels, 2006.

ILLUSTRATION CREDITS

We wish to acknowledge the following for providing the illustrations included in the book. Every effort has been made to locate the copyright holders for materials used, and we apologize for any oversights. Unless otherwise noted, all other images are from the author's collection.

AP/Wide World Photos: 9, 16, 17, 18 middle, 19, 21 bottom, 23, 25, 27 right, 29 top, 30 both, 31 bottom, 35 both, 40 left, 41 top, 43 bottom, 45 both, 47 top, 49, 51 bottom, 53 top right and bottom right, 55 top, 56 right, 57 right, 59 right, 61 both, 65 bottom, 66 top, 67, 68 top right, 69 top left, 69 bottom left and right, 73 bottom, 74 bottom, 75 top, 75 bottom right, 76 bottom right, 79 bottom, 81 bottom left, 85 both, 87, 90 bottom, 93, 95 both, 99, 101, 102, 103 bottom, 105 bottom, 106, 107 top, 109 both, 110, 111 left, 113 both, 118 top right, 121 bottom, 123 both, 124, 125 left, 126, 127 top right, 127 bottom right, 129 top, 131 both, 133 right, 135, 137 both, 139 bottom, 141 bottom.

Boston Public Library, Print Department, Herald-Traveler Photo Morgue: 47 bottom.

Boston Public Library, Print Department, Leslie Jones Collection: 36 top.

Boston Public Library, Print Department, McGreevey Collection: 11, 20, 26 top, 34 top, 44.

Boston Public Library, Print Department, Sports Images Collection: 29 bottom.

Chicago Historical Society: 31 top.

Culver Pictures: 70 top.

George Brace Photo Collection: 27 left, 36 bottom, 42 bottom, 52 bottom left, 80 both, 100 left.

Getty Images/Major League Baseball Photos/Michael Zagaris: 37, 39 bottom.

Library of Congress, Prints and Photographs Division: 8, 10 bottom, 14–15 top, 14 bottom, 40 right, 42–43 top, 64 top left, 70 bottom, 78, 84 left, 88 left, 96 bottom, 98 left, 112 top, 130.

Library of Congress, Prints and Photographs Division, George Grantham Bain Collection: 5, 12, 28 both, 34 bottom, 38 top left, 41 bottom, 50, 51 top, 58 bottom right, 60 bottom left, 63 all, 64 top right, 64 bottom left and right, 76 bottom left, 90 top, 103 top left, 116, 129 bottom, 133 left, 136 right, 138 left.

National Baseball Hall of Fame Library, Cooperstown, N.Y.: 18 bottom, 24 left, 32 both, 54 right, 56 left (courtesy Hillerich & Bradsby), 58 top right, 72 both, 73 top, 76 top, 79 top, 104 left, 106, 112 bottom, 118 left, 121 top, 122, 132, 134 top, 136 left, 139 top, 140 top.

Ponzini, Michael: 21 top right, 39 top, 89 bottom, 91, 97 left, 100 right, 115 left, 125 right.

Rickerby, Arthur: 24 right, 68 bottom, 86 bottom, 104 right, 105 top.

Sauritch, Lou: 13 top, 89 top.

Star Tribune **(Minneapolis)/Carlos Gonzalez:** 111 right.

Transcendental Graphics/The Rucker Archive: 21 top left, 22 both, 26 bottom, 38 top right, 38 bottom, 46, 48 both, 60 top, 62 all, 65 top left, 68 top left, 74 top, 82 both, 92, 94, 96 top, 118 bottom right, 127 left.

Tringali, Rob, Jr.: 59 left, 75 bottom left, 83 top left and right, 97 right.

Yablonsky, Bryan: 65 top right, 103 top right, 115 right, 117 bottom, 119 right.

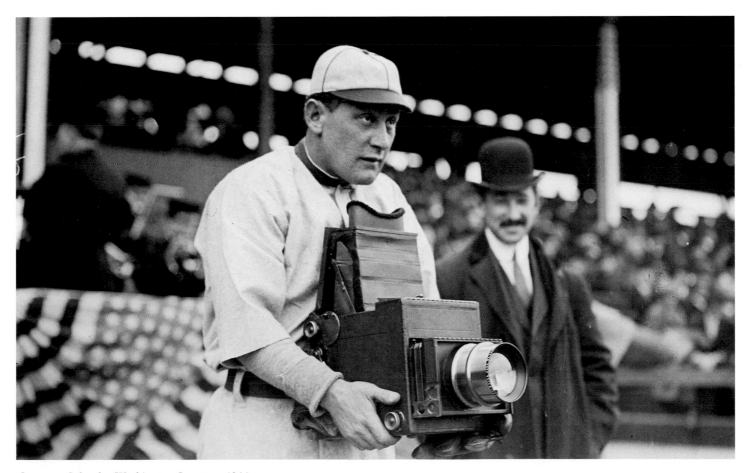

Germany Schaefer, Washington Senators, 1911

Contents

BASEBALL YESTERDAY, BASEBALL TODAY

The game of baseball as we know it today has existed in some form for two centuries. The foundation for the current system of rules was set 15 years before the start of the Civil War. Major league baseball's dual-league structure has been in place for over a hundred years. More than 50 North American cities have hosted major league teams since the first professional league, the National Association of Professional Base Ball Clubs, was formed in 1871. Since the foundation of the National League in 1876, more than 16,000 people, from nearly 50 countries, have participated in America's national pastime at the major league level. Add in players from the Negro Leagues and all levels of the minor league system, and tens of thousands more can be added to the all-time roster of professional ballplayers.

Throughout the sport's long and distinguished history, there have been dozens of changes to the official rules, from calling a foul ball a strike to the institution of the designated hitter. The game has moved indoors, onto artificial turf, and under artificial lights. We've gone from racially segregated leagues to a rich mix of ethnicities and nationalities. We've seen player strikes and lockouts, rumors of juiced balls and juiced batters, scandal and salvation. Through the home-run races and pennant chases, the sport has undergone innumerable modifications during the last century and a half. Yet one thing remains the same: It is still *baseball*.

Teams still field nine players at a time. The baseball diamond still consists of four bases placed at 90-foot intervals, and the pitcher

Batter Ichiro Suzuki, catcher Bengie Molina, and umpire Greg Gibson, 2004

still delivers the ball to a batter standing at home plate. The greats of the game will always loom larger than life, from Cy Young and Wee Willie Keeler to Pedro Martinez and Albert Pujols. We forever cheer on our hometown heroes and razz the opposition. And we can still enjoy a hot dog on a sunny July afternoon at the ballpark.

Poster of batter, catcher, and umpire, 1895

Elysian Fields in Hoboken, 1865

St. George Grounds, Staten Island, circa 1886

THE BALLPARK

One of the great things about baseball is that it can be played pretty much anywhere, given a field with enough open space—no goals or baskets or other structures are required. When the Knickerbocker Base Ball Club of New York, the first organized baseball team, went searching for just such a space, they headed across the Hudson River from Manhattan to Hoboken, New Jersey, to a spot known as Elysian Fields. The Knickerbockers came by ferry for practices and intra-squad matches. The first official game between two different clubs was played at Elysian Fields on June 19, 1846, when the New York Nine bested the host Knickerbockers by a score of 23-1. Elysian Fields remained the regular grounds for the Knickerbockers and other New York teams for many years. On August 3, 1865, a crowd gathered at Elysian Fields to watch the Brooklyn Atlantics and New York Mutuals face off in a "Grand Match for the Championship," as depicted in the Currier and Ives lithograph at left.

By the 1860s, as the popularity of the sport grew, teams began building enclosed ballparks and charging admission. In 1862, William Cammeyer converted his ice-skating rink in Williamsburg, Brooklyn, into the Union Grounds for baseball during the spring and summer months. He built a grandstand for the fans and surrounded the field with a six-foot fence to create the first enclosed ballpark. In the mid-1880s, the proprietors of the St. George Grounds in Staten Island touted the park's easy access from Manhattan and the benefits of spending a day in the fresh air.

Ballparks became larger and more elaborate during the 1880s and 1890s. The palatial "Grand Pavilion" of Boston's South End Grounds opened in 1888 as home to the Boston Beaneaters. Just six years later it fell victim to a common scourge of the wooden ballparks: fire. The grandstand and bleachers were reconstructed in a more modest version, which remained the home of the Beaneaters (later known as the Braves) until 1915.

South End Grounds, Boston, 1890

Shibe Park exterior, circa 1909

The emergence of steel-and-concrete ballparks after the turn of the twentieth century not only brought about more stable structures that were resistant to fire and collapse, but it also prompted renewed interest in building lavishly adorned baseball palaces. The first such palaces were Philadelphia's Shibe Park and Pittsburgh's Forbes Field, both of which opened in 1909. One of the grandest structures in all of sports, Shibe Park's rounded entrance tower and arched windows truly reflected the attention that was paid to creating a grand environment in which to experience the game of baseball. Ebbets Field in Brooklyn, built in 1913, was another classic example from the golden age of the ballpark. It has inspired many of the current crop of retro-style ballparks.

The spirit of these two legendary ballparks has been revived in cities around the country since the early 1990s. The team that started the trend back to classically styled stadiums was the Baltimore Orioles. The beautiful Oriole Park at Camden Yards, which opened in 1992, sparked others to build intimate, baseball-only ballparks that reflect the architecture and atmosphere of its neighborhood. Camden Yards' brick-and-stone exterior and arched windows are reminiscent of details from Shibe Park and Ebbets Field. The B&O Warehouse building behind right field further ties the ballpark to its surroundings and gives it a uniqueness that was lacking in stadiums of previous decades.

B&O Warehouse, Oriole Park at Camden Yards, 1992

Ebbets Field exterior

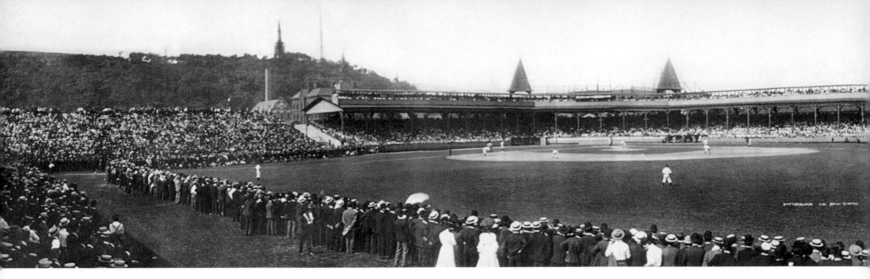

Exposition Park, 1905

Forbes Field entrance, 1909

EVOLUTION OF THE BALLPARK

The evolution of ballparks can be roughly divided into four principal eras: the wooden parks of the late-1800s; the steel-and-concrete "jewel boxes" of the 1910s and 1920s; the multipurpose, cookie-cutter stadiums of the 1960s and 1970s; and the retro-style revival of the late-twentieth and early twenty-first centuries. Along with Philadelphia and Cincinnati, few cities better illustrate this evolution than Pittsburgh.

Located along the banks of the Allegheny River, Exposition Park hosted baseball on and off from 1882 to 1915. It served as the home field for teams from five different professional leagues: the Allegheny club of the American Association (1882–1883), the Unions of the Union Association (1884), the Burghers of the Players League (1890), the Pirates of the National League (1891–1909), and the Rebels of the Federal League (1914–1915). Exposition Park's single-deck grandstand was topped by a row of skyboxes. Uncovered bleachers extended from the grandstand down the foul

Forbes Field, 1950s

lines and into the outfield. As was typical in the dead-ball era, hundreds of fans could watch the game from standing-room sections on the outfield grass. With dimensions of 450 feet to center field and 400 feet down the foul lines, Exposition Park had ample room to accommodate the capacity crowd of some 16,000 that attended the Pirates game against the New York Giants in August 1905, shown in the panoramic photo above.

In the middle of the 1909 baseball season, the Pittsburgh Pirates relocated to the steel-and-concrete Forbes Field. In addition to its two-tiered grandstand, this lavish park also featured the convenience of ramps for the spectators, elevators to the luxury boxes atop the grandstand, restroom attendants, telephones, dressing rooms for the umpires, and a clubhouse for each team. Forbes Field was expanded in 1925 from 23,000 to 41,000 seats by extending the double-deck grandstand around to right-center field. Lights were added for night baseball in 1940.

Forbes Field, 1910s

Three Rivers Stadium, Opening Day 1996

By the time that Forbes Field started to show its age in the late 1960s, the trend in ballpark construction was for enclosed, symmetrical stadiums—labeled "concrete doughnuts" by some—that could accommodate both baseball and football, as well as other events. Pittsburgh's Three Rivers Stadium was a quintessential example. From the artificial grass to the closed-off outfield, it lacked the charm and personality of its predecessors. Seats in the upper deck were a long way away from the action on the field, as is evident in the view from high up in Section 634 during Pittsburgh's 1996 opener seen above.

After 30 seasons at Three Rivers, the Pirates moved into one of the finest of the modern retro-style baseball fields in 2001. With only two seating levels, PNC Park recaptures the intimate environment found in the classic urban ballparks like Forbes, Ebbets Field, and others. It has a seating capacity of just over 38,000—compared to the 59,000 that Three Rivers could seat at its peak. The open outfield at PNC Park offers views of the downtown skyline and the Robert Clemente Bridge across the Allegheny River. The scoreboards reflect a mix of old and new, from the large video board above the left-field bleachers to the out-of-town scoreboard built into the right-field wall. Although the team failed to post a winning record in its first six seasons at PNC (and counting), the ballpark still drew a sellout crowd for the Pirates' home opener against the Dodgers in April 2006, as seen on the facing page.

PNC Park, Opening Day 2006

THE NAME GAME

When the earliest ballparks were built in the late 1800s, the names often came directly from the parks' locations; Chicago had West Side Grounds and South Side Park, and Boston's two teams played at the South End Grounds and the Huntington Avenue Grounds. A few ballpark names reflected a more enthusiastic spirit, such as the Palace of the Fans, a grand facility that opened in Cincinnati in 1902.

Gradually, the egos of the owners began to assert themselves. After all, in those days the men who owned the teams were responsible for building them a home as well. Between 1909 and 1913, Philadelphia's Ben Shibe, Brooklyn's Charles Ebbets, Chicago's

Briggs Stadium, Detroit

Charles Comiskey, and others constructed parks that bore their own names over the entrance. National Park in Washington became Griffith Stadium in 1920, renamed for owner Clark Griffith. When William Wrigley became the sole owner of the Chicago Cubs in 1919, he first changed the name of his stadium to Cubs Park, but in 1926 he rechristened it Wrigley Field. Frank Navin built Navin Field for his Detroit Tigers in 1912; when Walter Briggs took over the team in the 1930s, the park got a new name as well: Briggs Stadium. The club's third owner, John Fetzer, gave the ballpark a name it would bear for its final 30 seasons: Tiger Stadium.

By the end of the twentieth century, as the costs involved in building a new stadium reached astronomical levels, teams were looking for outside funding wherever they could get it. One

Comiskey Park, Chicago

Below: Palace of the Fans, Cincinnati

popular approach was to sell the name to the highest bidder. The Colorado Rockies were the first to follow this route, selling the name of their new ballpark in 1995 to the locally based Coors Brewing Company. Since then, major league ballparks have been named for everything from insurance agencies to pet-supply companies.

If stadium names used to change with each new team owner, the vagaries of corporate America have not made for stability in our ballparks either. In its first seven seasons alone, the home ballpark of the San Francisco Giants has been known by three differ-

ent names: first Pacific Bell Park, then SBC Park, and now (as of 2006, anyway) AT&T Park.

And then there was Enron Field. The Houston-based energy company had agreed to pay $100 million over 30 years for the naming rights to the Astros' new ballpark in 2000. After the company became embroiled in a financial scandal in 2001, the team bought back the name and called the stadium Astros Field. Less than two months into the 2002 season, the Astros announced a deal with the Minute Maid Company, worth reportedly $170 million, to name the ballpark Minute Maid Park for the next 28 years.

The ballpark formerly known as Enron Field, Houston

South End Grounds, 1888

THE BASEBALL DIAMOND

When Alexander Cartwright of the New York Knickerbockers laid out a set of rules for the game of baseball in 1845, he stipulated that the distance between home plate and second base and between first base and third base must be 42 paces. If one figures a pace to be equivalent to 3 feet, Cartwright's baseball diamond measures about 90 feet between the bases. This distance was formally entered into the rules following the first Convention of Base Ball Clubs in 1857. The 1867 edition of *Beadle's Dime Base-Ball Player*—the first published baseball guide—included a sketch of the field that specified 90 feet between bases. Although the pitcher's mound is not yet present, the infield diamond at South End Grounds in 1888, shown above, has the configuration that is familiar today.

The dimensions and basic shape of the baseball diamond have changed little over the past 150 years, but the advent of artificial turf and multipurpose stadiums in the 1960s and 1970s brought a radical new look to the playing field. The grass itself was fake—a travesty in the minds of traditionalists everywhere—and the dirt base paths were confined to the area surrounding the bases. Veterans Stadium in Philadelphia was typical of the cookie-cutter stadiums of that era.

During the late 1990s and early 2000s, artificial turf largely went the way of the dead ball and flannel uniforms. Today, only three major league parks feature artificial turf, compared to as many as 10 in the early 1980s.

Chase Field in Phoenix and Comerica Park in Detroit have brought back another old-time feature of early baseball diamonds: a dirt path between the pitcher's mound and home plate. This keyhole-shaped design was originally introduced so that the catcher wouldn't wear out the grass on his many trips back and forth to the mound, but it fell out of favor by the middle of the twentieth century. The Diamondbacks and Tigers revived it as an aesthetic feature that recalls an earlier day.

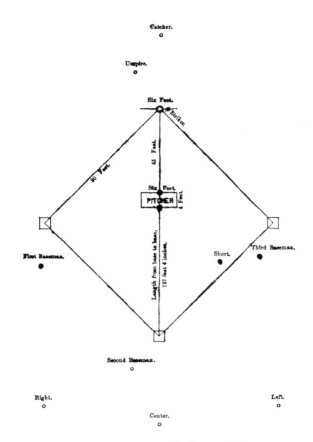

Above: Veterans Stadium, Philadelphia, 1994

Sketch from Beadle's Dime Base Ball Player, *1867*

Below: Chase Field, Arizona, 1998

THE PITCHER'S MOUND

The pitcher's mound did not officially become part of the baseball field until 1904. During the nineteenth century, the pitcher usually stood on level ground when delivering the ball to home plate. In the match between the Brooklyn Atlantics and the Cincinnati Red Stockings in 1870, depicted below from *Harper's Weekly*, the pitcher is delivering the ball from a flat pitcher's box (and using an underhand delivery, as was the regulation at the time).

The pitcher (or "thrower," as he was then known) also stood closer to the batter ("striker") than he does today. No specific distance was listed in the 1845 Knickerbocker Rules, but the Convention of Base Ball Clubs in 1857 established that the pitcher must stand at least 45 feet from the batter. The diamond diagram in the 1881 edition of the *Spalding Baseball Guide* shows the revised distance of 50 feet, which was adopted that season by the National League to "increase the batting." The pitching distance was altered one more time, in 1893, when it was decreed that the pitcher must stand 60 feet, 6 inches from home plate, which has remained the standard ever since.

Another rule instituted in 1893 was the introduction of the pitching plate, a 12-inch-by-4-inch rubber slab. Prior to that, the pitcher had to throw from within a pitcher's box, the dimensions of which changed several times, varying from a long and narrow 12 feet by 3 feet to a square 6-foot box. The rubber was enlarged to 24 inches by 6 inches in 1895, the dimensions it holds to this day.

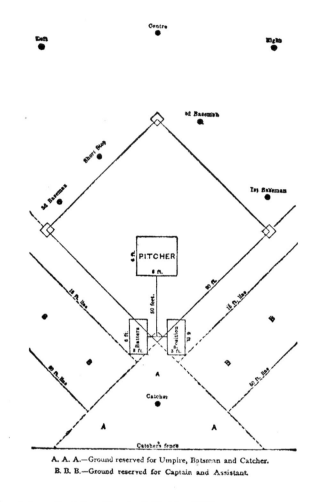

Sketch from Spalding Baseball Guide, *1881*

Below: Brooklyn Atlantics vs. Cincinnati Red Stockings, 1870

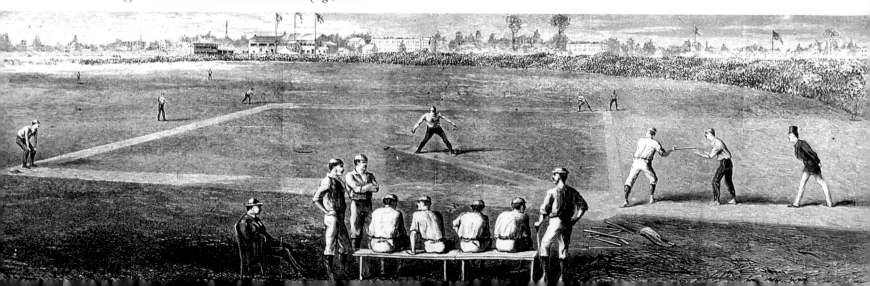

Bob Gibson on the mound, 1968 World Series

When the pitcher's mound was introduced in 1904, the maximum height was set at 15 inches, although some grounds crews were rumored to have added a few inches to give an extra edge to the pitcher. Despite having the high ground, literally, major league pitchers were pounded with record-high levels of runs during the 1920s and 1930s. By the mid-1960s, pitchers started to regain the upper hand. The pitcher's edge was most evident in 1968, the so-called Year of the Pitcher, when teams scored an average of 3.4 runs per game, the second-lowest in baseball history. St. Louis' Bob Gibson led the way with a 1.12 ERA—the lowest ERA since 1914 and the fourth-best ever—and he struck out a record 17 Detroit Tiger batters in the opening game of that year's World Series. Major League Baseball responded by lowering the mound five inches the very next season. Even as the combined ERA of the league has hovered above 4.00 for well over a decade, the mound height has not wavered from the 10-inch level established in 1968.

THE BULLPEN

There are many theories about how the bullpen got its name. Some say that it came from the Bull Durham tobacco billboards that stood above where the pitchers warmed up in one or more ballparks. Another theory is that the fenced-in area is reminiscent of the pen where bulls are kept before being released into the ring.

Whatever the reason for the name, the bullpen areas in old-time parks tended to be rudimentary spaces. They usually offered little more than a bench to sit on and, for the lucky ones, a roof over head, tucked away in foul territory or deep in the outfield. Forbes Field was known as a pitcher-friendly ballpark, but the bullpens were not particularly inviting. In the photo at right Pittsburgh's Roy Face is getting loose before the start of a 1960 World Series game in a sparse bullpen in the right-field corner.

Today's bullpens range from simple benches in foul territory to private waiting areas behind the outfield wall. Some ballparks have incorporated bi-level bullpens that offer better viewing by and of the pitchers during the game. At Angel Stadium of Anaheim (seen in the photo at far right), the home-team staff sits in the lower, field-level pen—allowing this bullpen coach to snare a Troy Glaus home run during the 2002 World Series, as the Giants relievers look on helplessly from the upper-tier bullpen behind.

Harvey Haddix in the Forbes Field bullpen, 1960 World Series

At Citizens Bank Park in Philadelphia, a special platform on the concourse provides fans with an up-close-and-personal look into the bi-level bullpens. Of course, this access isn't always so nice for the visiting team. Philadelphia's notoriously vocal fans can give an earful of abuse to the pitchers loosening up in the upper bullpen. (At first the Phillies pitchers were given the upper bullpen, but when even they began hearing it from the fans, they moved to the lower pen closer to the field.)

Bull Durham tobacco billboard

Bullpen at Angel Stadium of Anaheim, 2002 World Series

Huntington Avenue Grounds, 1903

Babe Ruth unconscious, Griffith Stadium, 1931

THE OUTFIELD WALL

While outfield fences often served little purpose in keeping the ball inside the park during the dead-ball era, keeping the nonpaying masses out of the park was a concern for team owners. The wooden fences of early ballparks usually were built tall, but determined fans with a helping hand often found a way to beat the system, as shown in the scene outside of Boston's Huntington Avenue Grounds before the 1903 World Series (left).

The shift from wood to steel and concrete materials in ballpark construction beginning in the 1910s greatly reduced the risk of fire—while introducing a new hazard for the players. When Babe Ruth chased down a fly ball at Washington's Griffith Stadium in 1931, he learned the hard way that the concrete walls were not as forgiving as the wooden ones.

By the 1940s, many teams began to add padding to the outfield walls. The cushioned walls of modern ballparks offer more than just a safety feature for today's athletic outfielders. Rather than fans climbing the walls from the outside in search of a better view of the game, it's the fielders who scale the fences in search of dramatic catches. Milwaukee's Carlos Lee (shown in the photo at right) dug his cleats into the soft padding at the new Busch Stadium in April

Carlos Lee, 2006

Grounds crew planting ivy at Wrigley Field, 1937

2006 to get a little extra elevation and snare a would-be home run off the bat of St. Louis' David Eckstein.

At Chicago's Wrigley Field, however, foliage is still the only thing protecting the fielders from the hard brick wall around much of the outfield. The ivy was the brainchild of pioneering baseball executive Bill Veeck while he was with the Cubs in the 1930s.

Matty McIntyre at Hilltop Park

BILLBOARDS

As much as the modern fan might bemoan the excessive corporate sponsorship of our national pastime, baseball owners and businessmen a century ago also recognized the commercial opportunities available in the vast real estate of a ballpark. Local and national companies alike posted huge billboards hawking everything from beer and cigarettes to underwear and automobile tires. In the photo above, a wall full of ads at New York's Hilltop Park provides the backdrop as White Sox outfielder Matty McIntyre warms up before a game,

circa 1910. The front of the bleacher section at the Polo Grounds in 1921 (seen below left) was framed by ads for Boston Garters and Hole-Proof Hosiery—after all, what says "baseball" more than ladies' undergarments?

Fenway Park's towering Green Monster in left field is one of the most distinctive features of any ballpark, but the monster wasn't always green. Before 1947, the 37-foot wall was covered with billboard ads just like at any ballpark. Gem Razors was a common sponsor at baseball fields around the country in the mid-twentieth century.

In ballparks today, advertising goes beyond just the outfield wall and now adorns nearly every available surface. A combination of local, national, and multi-national companies pay big bucks for the opportunity to display their name in front of hundreds of thousands of fans over a full season. Innovations such as the electronic billboard and the trivision billboard allow ads to change during the course of a game. Advertisements are also becoming more integrated into the playing field. That's not a car parked in the Shea Stadium outfield in the photo above right, but San Diego's Dave Roberts almost blends in with this lifelike ad while making a leaping catch during a Mets-Padres contest in 2005.

Billboards at the Polo Grounds, 1921

Left: Billboard at Shea Stadium, 2005

Below: Billboards on the Green Monster, 1942

THE SCOREBOARD

More than any other sport, baseball is a game of numbers, and no baseball field is complete without a scoreboard to record those numbers for all to see. The earliest ballparks posted the inning-by-inning score manually on chalkboards or using wooden planks with numbers printed on them. The two young scorekeepers at South Side Park, home of the Chicago White Sox from 1901 until 1910, had to climb precariously placed ladders to keep the score up-to-the-minute.

The first electronic scoreboard was invented by George Baird in 1908, and it included lights to record balls, strikes, and outs. Crosley Field in Cincinnati had a large scoreboard in left field that featured electric lights above the line score to indicate strikes, balls, and outs, as well as to let fans know whether a play was scored a

Ameriquest Field manual scoreboard, 2006

hit or an error. The inning-by-inning score, the lineups for both teams, and scores from select games around the league were updated manually. In 1957, Crosley's original scoreboard was replaced by an even larger one that measured 58 feet high by 65 feet wide.

The electronic age came to scoreboards in 1980 when the Los Angeles Dodgers became the first to install a video-display board. Since then, scoreboards and video boards throughout the league have become elaborate gizmos that show instant replays, video highlights from around the league, detailed stats, and advertisements throughout the game. Jacobs Field in Cleveland features a massive, 149-foot-long by 36-foot-tall, light emitting diode (LED) video board in left field, the largest in baseball. Another innovation at "the Jake" is the 172-foot-long LED out-of-town scoreboard built into the outfield fence.

As twenty-first-century stadiums expand their high-tech offerings, many retro-style parks have sought to incorporate elements of the old ballparks as well. Within the left-field wall at Ameriquest Field in Arlington, Texas, an old-style manual scoreboard keeps tabs on games around the league. In the photo above, the scorekeeper peers through an opening next to the Minnesota-Chicago score to watch Kevin Mench field a fly ball during a Rangers game against Tampa Bay in April 2006.

Crosley Field scoreboard, 1949

Left: South Side Park scoreboard, 1905

Below: Jacobs Field video board, 2005

THE SCORECARD

Even as scoreboards and video boards at the ballpark present the fan with a bewildering array of stats and facts about the game's progress, keeping score remains a popular activity for fans of all ages. Scorecards were in use by both official scorers and dedicated fans as early as the 1850s. The scorecard shown below from a game involving the Mears Base Ball Club around 1860 shows an assortment of symbols and notations that are hardly recognizable to the modern fan. In 1863, Henry Chadwick developed a detailed scoring system to record the results of every at bat. He assigned numerical symbols for each position on the field as well as a series of abbreviations for every possible outcome of a plate appearance. Chadwick's system has been greatly expanded and modified over the years to keep up with baseball's increasing thirst for statistical information and detail, but his rules of scoring remain the foundation for any amateur or professional scorer.

Scorecard cover, Brooklyn Bridegrooms, 1897

Scorecard, 1860

THE BOX SCORE

Baseball box scores have been appearing in newspapers for nearly as long as organized teams have been playing the game. The box score from the Buffalo *Courier* of October 6, 1896, shows the results of the third game of the Temple Cup championship between the Baltimore Orioles and the Cleveland Spiders. It includes many elements that fans more than a century later might expect to see in the morning paper. (The abbreviation "B.H." for batted hits is now abbreviated simply as "H.") You won't find any tally of RBI, however, since runs batted in was not introduced into official scoring until 1920. The pitchers' stat line is also just a brief summary, rather than the full boxes we see today.

As statistical analyses have increased exponentially over the decades, the amount of information contained in the box score has increased to nearly the same degree. In addition to RBI, new statistical notations such as GIDP (grounding into double plays) and BS (blown save) would be meaningless to fans of Henry Chadwick's era. But even with the depths of statistical detail, the box score cannot fully convey the significance—or controversy—behind the notation "Bonds (6)" in the San Francisco Giants' 4-2 victory over the Oakland A's on May 20, 2006. It was the 714th home run of Barry Bonds' career, tying him with the immortal Babe Ruth on the all-time list.

BALTIMORE WINS AGAIN.

Cuppy and Hoffer Both Do Effective Work— Series Continued on Wednesday.

Baltimore, Oct. 5.—The chances for the Temple Cup resting in Baltimore this winter are very bright. To-day the third game of the series with the Cleveland team, and the last one to be played in Baltimore, went to the home team by the score of 6 to 2. The champions need but one more game to capture the cup.

The teams will continue the series in Cleveland on Wednesday. This afternoon's contest was remarkable for the number of brilliant catches in the outfield, and the small number of assists. Hoffer was not as effective as on last Friday, and his loyal rooters were in a constant state or worriment for five innings. He was a tower of strength in the last four innings, and only one single was tallied by the Clevelands.

Cuppy pitched a brilliant game up to the eighth inning when the champions fell on him for three singles and a double, scoring three runs. Attendance 4,200. Score:

BALTIMORE.	A.B.	R.	B.H.	P.O.	A.	E.
McGraw, 3b	4	2	2	2	1	0
Keeler, r. f.	4	1	1	1	0	0
Jennings, s. s.	4	0	0	2	7	1
Kelley, l. f.	4	0	2	4	0	0
Doyle, 1b	4	1	0	5	0	1
Reitz, 2b	4	0	0	5	0	0
Brodie, c. f.	4	0	1	0	0	0
Robinson, c.	4	1	1	8	1	0
Hoffer, p.	3	1	1	0	1	0
Totals	35	6	8	27	10	2
CLEVELAND.	A.B.	R.	B.H.	P.O.	A.	E.
Burkett, l. f.	5	1	2	7	0	0
McKean, s. s.	5	0	1	3	3	0
Childs, 2b	4	1	1	2	0	0
McAleer, c. f.	4	0	2	3	0	0
O'Connor, 1b	4	0	2	5	0	0
Zimmer, c.	4	0	1	3	0	1
McGarr, 3b	4	0	0	2	1	1
Blake, r. f.	4	0	1	2	0	0
Cuppy, p.	4	0	0	0	1	0
Totals	38	2	10	27	5	2

Baltimore .... 0 1 1 0 0 1 0 3 0—6
Cleveland .... 0 0 1 0 1 0 0 0 0—2

Earned runs—Baltimore 5, Cleveland 1. First base by errors—Cleveland 2. Left on bases—Baltimore 2, Cleveland 10. First base on balls—Off Hoffer 1. Struck out—By Hoffer 5, by Cuppy 2. Three-base hit—Hoffer. Two-base hit—Robinson. Stolen bases—Doyle, McGraw 2, Keeler. Umpires—Sheridan and Emslie. Time—2 hours.

Box score from Temple Cup championship, 1896

GIANTS 4, ATHLETICS 2

San Fran	AB	R	H	BI	BB	SO	Avg.
Winn rf	5	0	1	0	0	0	.283
Vizquel ss	3	1	2	0	2	0	.293
Feliz 3b	5	1	1	0	0	1	.275
Bonds dh	3	1	1	1	2	1	.229
1-Ortmeier pr-dh	0	0	0	0	0	0	.286
Durham 2b	5	0	2	1	0	0	.229
SFinley cf	4	0	1	1	0	0	.291
Matheny c	5	1	1	1	0	1	.252
MaSweeney 1b	3	0	1	0	1	1	.253
JVizcaino 1b	1	0	0	0	0	0	.170
Ellison lf	3	0	1	0	0	0	.278
Totals	37	4	11	4	5	4	
Oakland	AB	R	H	BI	BB	SO	Avg.
Ellis 2b	5	1	1	0	0	0	.252
Swisher lf	5	0	0	0	0	1	.293
Kotsay cf	4	0	2	0	1	0	.293
EChavez 3b	4	1	1	1	1	0	.290
Thomas dh	4	0	0	0	0	0	.178
Crosby ss	4	0	1	0	0	1	.241
Payton rf	4	0	2	1	0	0	.258
Kendall c	4	0	0	0	0	1	.267
DJohnson 1b	4	0	2	0	0	1	.196
2-APerez pr	0	0	0	0	0	0	.040
Totals	38	2	9	2	2	4	

San Fran	010	000	100	2—4	11 0
Oakland	100	000	001	0—2	9 0

1-ran for Bonds in the 10th. 2-ran for Johnson in the 10th. **LOB**—San Francisco 10, Oakland 8. **2B**—Vizquel (6), DJohnson (5). **HR**—Matheny (3), off Halsey; Bonds (6), off Halsey. **RBIs**—Bonds (15), Durham (14), SFinley (18), Matheny (16), EChavez (29), Payton (9). **SB**—Payton (2). **S**—Ellison. **SF**—SFinley. **GIDP**—Winn, Durham. **Runners left in scoring position**—San Francisco 4 (Winn, Feliz, Bonds, JVizcaino); Oakland 4 (Swisher, EChavez, Crosby, DJohnson). **Runners moved up**—Ellis. **DP**—San Francisco 1 (Feliz); Oakland 2 (Crosby, Ellis and DJohnson), (EChavez, Ellis and DJohnson).

San Francisco	IP	H	R	ER	BB	SO	NP	ERA
Schmidt	8⅓	7	2	2	1	3	132	3.07
Bnitez W, 3-0 BS,2	1⅔	2	0	0	1	1	27	0.00
Oakland	IP	H	R	ER	BB	SO	NP	ERA
Halsey	6⅓	6	2	2	2	4	93	3.15
Keisler	1⅔	2	0	0	1	0	24	2.08
Calero L, 0-1	1	2	2	2	0	1	24	6.46
Karsay	1	1	0	0	0	0	7	2.70

Keisler pitched to 1 batter in the 9th, Calero pitched to 3 batters in the 10th. **Inherited runners-scored**—Benitez 2-1, Keisler 1-0, Calero 1-0, Karsay 3-2. **IBB**—off Calero (Bonds) 1, off Keisler (Bonds) 1. **Umpires**—Home, Rick Reed; First, Tim Tschida; Second, Ted Barrett; Third, Troy Fullwood. **T**—3:22. **A**—35,077 (34,077).

Box score from Giants-A's game, May 20, 2006

Dugout at Huntington Avenue Grounds, 1903 World Series

THE DUGOUT

In 1903, the National League Champion Pittsburgh Pirates didn't enjoy much in the way of dugout luxuries at Boston's Huntington Avenue Grounds during the first World Series. Indeed, the presence of walls and a roof was an upgrade from the open benches on which teams sat in ballparks of the late 1800s, exposed to the flying barbs and occasional flying bottle from rowdy fans.

As dugouts became more permanent structures along the base of the ballpark grandstands, they still lacked storage space for the players' equipment. Throughout much of the first half of the twentieth century, teams laid their bats directly in front of the dugout steps. To eliminate this on-field obstacle, bat racks began appearing in dugouts by the 1930s.

Simple benches remain the standard seating option in most dugouts today. In more luxurious parks, the seating might be padded, as in the forward row of benches in San Francisco's spacious dugout at AT&T Park. Additional amenities include racks for the equipment and a plentiful supply of Gatorade and sunflower seeds—which litter the dugout floor by the end of a Giants-Cardinals game in May 2006.

Dugout at Yankee Stadium, 1923

While bats and gloves and masks no longer litter the front of the dugout, the fielders still have to navigate certain obstacles. The padded fence in front can't save Giants Mike Matheny and Lance Niekro from tumbling into the dugout while chasing down a foul ball at Miller Park in Milwaukee.

Left: Dugout at Miller Park, 2006

Below: Dugout at AT&T Park, 2006

Above: Clubhouse at Fenway Park, circa 1932

Left: Clubhouse at Comiskey Park, circa 1936

Clubhouse at McAfee Coliseum, 2004

THE CLUBHOUSE

Before 1906, ballplayers usually dressed into their uniforms at a hotel and were driven to the ballpark in horse-drawn carriages. Brooklyn's Charles Ebbets helped put an end to this practice of parading teams through the streets by encouraging the league to require all ballparks to have clubhouses for the home and visiting teams, complete with lockers and hot and cold running water. A state-of-the-art facility when it opened in 1912, Fenway Park's clubhouse counted among its amenities lockers for every player, stools to sit on, and a dedicated heating system. In this photo from the early 1930s, team trainer Bits Bierhalter makes sure that the Red Sox players stay warm as he stokes the clubhouse hot stove. The visitors' clubhouse is neatly arranged at Comiskey Park in the mid-1930s (bottom left).

The twenty-first-century ballplayer probably doesn't realize how good he has it. The plush leather couches, multiple televisions, and video arcade games make the clubhouse at Oakland's McAfee Coliseum feel more like a rec room than a locker room.

Honus Wagner, 1914

Satchel Paige, 1942

KEEPING FIT, STAYING HEALTHY

edicine balls, stationary bikes, and a good-old rubdown might seem quaint by modern standards, but if it was good enough for Honus Wagner, Babe Ruth, and Satchel Paige—three all-time greats—there must be something to it. Wagner was well known for his physical fitness and conditioning, and he remained active as a player until the age of 43. Ruth may be more commonly associated with hot dogs and beer in popular lore, but his dominance was founded largely on sheer strength and fitness. The final home run of Ruth's career was a towering shot onto the roof at Forbes Field in Pittsburgh, reportedly the farthest one ever hit at that ballpark; the Babe was 40 years old at the time. Though Leroy "Satchel" Paige preferred to keep his true age hidden, he didn't get his start in the major leagues until he was in his forties, after more than two decades as a legend of the Negro Leagues. As a pitcher with the Kansas City Monarchs in 1942, Paige receives some pregame treatment from team trainer Frank Floyd (above right).

Illegal performance-enhancing drugs notwithstanding, the potential for long and healthy careers has only improved with the access to state-of-the-art exercise equipment, dedicated personal trainers, personal dieticians, and a plethora of (legal) vitamin supplements. The stationary bike at Oakland's spring training facility in Phoenix is a space-age version of what Ruth pedaled 70 years earlier.

Of course, even with all the sophisticated equipment and carefully monitored conditioning regimes, it seems there will always be a place in baseball for the more, shall we say, full-figured athlete—as exhibited by Cecil Fielder, circa 1990, when he hit 51 homers.

Babe Ruth, 1926

Left: Cecil Fielder, 1990

Below: Oakland A's spring training facility, 2005

TAKE ME OUT TO THE BALLGAME

Tens of thousands of adults and children alike will stand in long lines, through all kinds of weather, to witness baseball's best showcase their talents and skills on the diamond. By 1924, Washington baseball fans had been waiting for nearly a quarter-century for a chance to see their Senators play in the World Series. Hopeful ticket buyers (seen near right) tried to get comfortable for an overnight stay out-

Fans at Griffith Stadium, 1924

Fans at Busch Stadium, 2004

side of Griffith Stadium more than 24 hours before tickets were to go on sale for Game 1.

Cardinals fans in 2004 came to Busch Stadium prepared for the long wait for playoff tickets, equipped with lawn chairs, coolers, and tents. It proved to be worth the wait, as St. Louis went on to win its first National League pennant in 17 years.

According to baseball historian Harold Seymour, the average admission price to a baseball game between 1909 and 1916 was 66 cents; individual tickets ranged from 25 cents for a spot in the bleachers to as much as $1.50 for a box seat. In the early 1900s, Brooklyn fans lined up outside of Washington Park to buy field-level tickets at a quarter a piece (below right).

The average ticket price for a regular-season game in 2006 was $22.21. Factor in the cost of parking, souvenirs, and food, a family of four can expect to spend more than $170 at a major league game. The oldest ballpark in the majors is also the most expensive ticket. The average price for a seat at Fenway Park in 2006 was $46.46; the front-row seats atop the Green Monster in left field go for $110 to $130 per game. Undaunted by the hefty price tag, Red Sox fans line up outside of Fenway on a chilly December morning in 2004 to purchase tickets for the 2005 season (above right).

Fans at Fenway Park, 2004

Fans at Washington Park, Brooklyn, early 1900s

In the nascent years of professional baseball, when ballparks had seating for only a few thousand spectators, teams were able to accommodate the growing number of fans, and bring in some extra income, by allowing people to stand or sit along the outskirts of the playing field. At an early incarnation of the Polo Grounds in New York in 1905 (above), fans arriving in horse-drawn carriages and motorcars share a makeshift parking lot beyond the ring of fans in the outfield. Even as ballparks got bigger and baseballs got livelier, teams would still pack fans onto the field for big games, as shown in the photo at right from Wrigley Field in 1937.

Modern ballparks have devised new and unique ways for fans to experience the game. At Arizona's Chase Field, the Pool Zone suite in right-center field includes a swimming pool and spa, a private bar, a television, and clear views of the action. All this and more is available to you, and 34 of your closest friends, for just under $6,000 a game. The view is similar to that afforded from the Polo Grounds' outfield a hundred years earlier—although you don't need to worry about where to park your horse.

Wrigley Field, Opening Day 1937

Above: The Polo Grounds, 1905   *Below: The Pool Zone at Chase Field, 2005*

Boston's Royal Rooters, 1903 World Series

THE FANS

Many cities can lay claim to having the most rabid fans, but the most renowned band of boosters in the early 1900s was the Royal Rooters of Boston. Initially supporters of the National League's Beaneaters, they switched allegiances to the Americans (Red Sox) in 1901—whose tickets happened to be cheaper. During the 1903 World Series at Huntington Avenue Grounds, the Rooters sat in a special roped-off area behind home plate, a prime spot from where they could cheer for their team, sing songs, and heckle the opposing Pirates. Pittsburgh's third baseman, Tommy Leach, said the Royal Rooters deserved some of the credit for Boston winning the World Series.

Although watching a major league game from the field is strictly off-limits these days—indeed, any attempt to come onto the field likely will result in arrest, as an eager Derek Jeter suitor learned at Yankee Stadium in 2002 (below right)—fans still find many ways to express their support for the home team. In St. Louis in 2000, a Cardinals supporter chooses to focus his disdain on the visiting New York Mets (above right).

Despite the increasing costs to attend a baseball game, fans are coming out to the ballpark at record numbers. Just short of 75 million people went (or bought a ticket, at least) to a Major League Baseball game in 2005, for an average attendance of 30,724 per game. The top five clubs (Yankees, Dodgers, Cardinals, Angels, and Giants) alone drew 17,819,039 fans in 2005; 50 years earlier, the entire league of 16 teams drew 16,617,383 fans to baseball games in 1955.

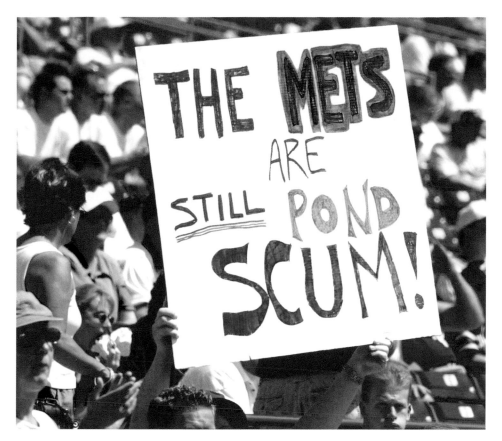

Left: Cardinals fan, 2004

Below: Fan nabbed by security at Yankee Stadium, 2002

Lakefront Park, 1883

LUXURY BOXES AND BLEACHER BUMS

Henry Chadwick remarked in the 1860s that charging admission to games would help to keep out the "blackguard boys and roughs," but baseball parks have long provided accommodations for fans from all classes. The 1883 sketch of Lakefront Park in Chicago (above) shows a row of private boxes atop the main grandstand for the upper echelons of the baseball-watching public—the sport's first "skyboxes," complete with armchairs and curtains. The masses, meanwhile, were free to cheer rowdily from the bleacher seats in the outfield. For some, bleacher freedom means going shirtless on a hot summer's day, as with this group of fans at the Fenway Park bleachers in 1951 (right).

Luxury boxes have become an essential revenue source for teams in the twenty-first century. Every new ballpark includes a number of private suites that can be sold to wealthy corporate sponsors. Teams such as the Cubs and Red Sox have renovated their historic homes to include more boxes and bring in additional income without having to build a new stadium. Rogers Centre in Toronto, which opened in 1989 as SkyDome, has 161 skyboxes, each carrying a price tag of about $200,000.

A more budget-conscious option is available at Coors Field in Colorado. Bleacher seating in the Rockpile goes for $4 for adults and $1 for kids under 12 and seniors over 55. The fresh mountain air and views of downtown Denver are included in the price.

Left: Rogers Centre, 2006

Below: Fenway Park bleachers, 1951

President Harry S. Truman at Griffith Stadium, 1950

PRESIDENTIAL FIRST PITCHES

O f all the esteemed spectators that attend baseball games, few elicit as much attention as the president of the United States—the "first fan." On April 10, 1910, President William Howard Taft inaugurated a tradition when he threw out the ceremonial first pitch of the season to Walter Johnson, star hurler and Opening Day starter for the Washington Senators. Taft was back at the ballpark to kick off the 1911 season. He had to miss the 1912 opener, however, when the sinking of the *Titanic* a day earlier superseded his baseball obligations. Vice President James S. Sherman took over the ceremonial task at the ballpark.

Every president from Taft through Richard M. Nixon pitched at least one ceremonial first ball at a Washington Senators opener during his administration. Not surprisingly, four-term-president Franklin D. Roosevelt made the most appearances (eight) at Griffith Stadium's Opening Day festivities in Washington.

President William H. Taft at American League Park, 1910

Harry S. Truman never missed an Opening Day during his presidency. The southpaw from Missouri was also the first commander-in-chief to deliver the season-opening pitch as a lefty, and in 1950, he went a step further and threw two first pitches: one left-handed and one right-handed.

When the Senators franchise left Washington in 1971, presidents took their show on the road. Presidents Ronald Reagan, George H. W. Bush, and Bill Clinton all traveled to Baltimore's Opening Day for the ceremony. In 1993, Clinton showed off his pitching arm and became the first president to throw from the mound to the catcher behind home plate, 60 feet 6 inches away.

Through the first six years of his presidency, George W. Bush delivered ceremonial pitches in four different ballparks. In 2005 he honored Major League Baseball's return to the nation's capital by throwing out the first pitch at the home opener for the Washington Nationals at R.F.K. Stadium. Bush's other ceremonial first pitches took place at the first-ever game at Miller Park, in 2001; at Busch Stadium, St. Louis, in 2004; and at Cincinnati's Great American Ballpark in 2006.

President George W. Bush at R.F.K. Stadium, 2004

TAKE ME *CLOSE* TO THE BALLGAME

For those unable to get a ticket to the big game, a little resourcefulness can provide a unique view of the action. In the photo to the right, taken outside of Pittsburgh's Exposition Park in 1909, adventurous fans climb a lamppost for a sneak peak into the World Series matchup between the Pirates and Detroit Tigers.

In cities such as Philadelphia and Chicago, people who lived across from their neighborhood ballparks could watch a game simply by opening the window shades. Residents of Twentieth Street across from Shibe Park went so far as to build makeshift bleachers on top of the buildings, charging admission and selling food and drinks. The rooftops were overflowing for the 1910 World Series, as shown in the photo at far right. The Philadelphia A's management didn't appreciate their neighbors undercutting the team's ticket sales, and in the mid-1930s, owner Connie Mack extended the height of the outfield wall to 33 feet, thus blocking out the views from the "wildcat bleachers" across the street. The new wall, dubbed the "spite fence," created a rift between the team and the fans that lasted until the A's left the city in 1954.

In Chicago, residents on Waveland and Sheffield streets across from Wrigley Field also have a long tradition of taking advantage of the rooftop views to catch the Cubbies free of charge. The enterprising building owners soon saw this as a money-making opportunity for themselves as well. They built permanent bleacher sections and began serving beer to paying customers, as seen in the photo of a game in July 2001. Peeved at this development, the Cubs installed a screen above the Wrigley Field bleachers in 2002 and 2003 to block out the views, but they soon came to a revenue-sharing agreement with the owners of the rooftop bleachers, and the harmony between the team and its neighbors remains strong.

Pittsburgh fans at the World Series, 1909

Rooftop bleachers across from Shibe Park, 1910

Rooftop bleachers across from Wrigley Field, 2001

Vendors at Briggs Stadium, 1930s

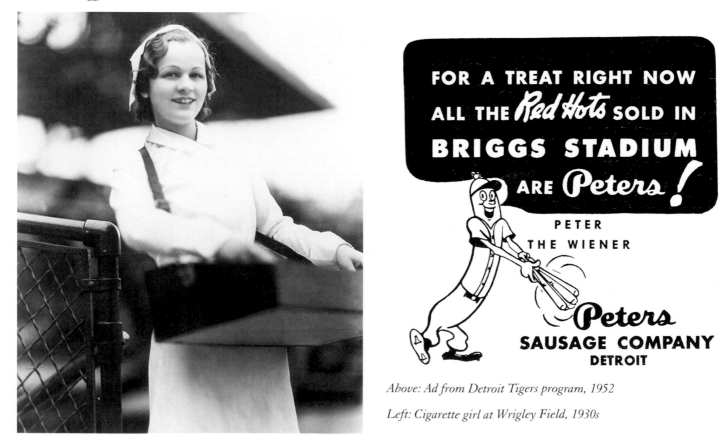

FOR A TREAT RIGHT NOW
ALL THE *Red Hots* SOLD IN
BRIGGS STADIUM
ARE *Peters*!

PETER
THE WIENER

Peters
SAUSAGE COMPANY
DETROIT

Above: Ad from Detroit Tigers program, 1952

Left: Cigarette girl at Wrigley Field, 1930s

FOOD AT THE BALLPARK

ot dogs, peanuts, popcorn, Cracker Jack, and other snacks have been ballpark staples for about as long as vendors and concessionaires have been offering food and drink at baseball games. Harry Stevens started selling ice cream, lemonade, and other refreshments at New York's Polo Grounds in the 1880s, and he is credited with popularizing "red hot sausages" on buns to the ballpark menu. In the early 1900s, vendors could be found strolling the aisles and along the front row of seats hawking snacks, beverages, scorecards, and more. In the photo at left the vendors at Briggs Stadium in Detroit are ready to serve up ice-cold Cokes, warm peanuts, and other treats to spectators at a Tigers game in the 1930s. While more and more stadiums these days are strictly nonsmoking, back in the day, "cigarette girls" sold packs right in the aisles at Wrigley Field and elsewhere.

Beer and hot dogs remain the biggest-selling items at sports arenas, but today the options are vast and varied from city to city. Concessions concourses are filled with offerings of cuisines from all around the world. At AT&T Park in San Francisco, ravenous fans

Hot dog vendor at Shea Stadium, 2003

Tacos stand at AT&T Park, 2003

can enjoy anything from crab cakes to tacos as they quaff fine wines and microbrews. In addition to the traditional concessions stands and vendors walking the aisles, many ballparks include food stalls in mall-like areas around the park. Former players are even getting into the restaurateur act, especially in the realm of barbecue: Boog Powell's Boog's Barbecue at Camden Yards in Baltimore, Greg "The Bull" Luzinski's Bull's BBQ at Citizens Bank Park in Philadelphia, and Manny Sanguillen's Manny's Bar-B-Q at PNC Park in Pittsburgh.

Add to the fun of watching the game.

you'll enjoy the high quality favorites served at Wrigley Field.

* Pabst Blue Ribbon Beer...*Now the Original is Here*
* Oscar Mayer *Yellow Band* Wieners...mild, tender, juicy
* Coca-Cola...Get a lift that you can feel...Swing to the Real Thing
* Hamm's Beer..."From The Land of Sky Blue Waters"
* Borden's Frostick...A frozen dairy food—chocolate coated

Food offerings at Wrigley Field, 1962

THE BALL

A rticle 1.09 of the Official Rules of Major League Baseball states: "The ball shall be a sphere formed by yarn wound around a small core of cork, rubber, or similar material, covered with two strips of white horsehide or cowhide, tightly stitched together. It shall weigh not less than 5 nor more than 5 1/4 ounces avoirdupois and measure not less than 9 nor more than 9 1/4 inches in circumference." Although theories emerge every few years about livelier baseballs, the official requirements have stood basically unchanged since 1872. (The more widely available cowhide was added to the list of acceptable cover materials in 1974.)

Official American League baseball, 1939

Albert G. Spalding's Chicago-based sporting goods company was the exclusive supplier of baseballs for the National League beginning in 1877, and Spalding's subsidiary, A. J. Reach, became the official American League supplier in 1901. The ball was made with a hard rubber center until 1910, when the cork center was introduced, on the suggestion of Philadelphia Athletics owner Ben Shibe. Cork was more durable and gave the ball more bounce. The prevalence of spitballs and scuff balls conspired to keep offenses in check for the remainder of the 1910s, but after trick pitches were banned in 1920—and as Babe Ruth's home run power was unleashed on the league—the dead-ball era came to a definite end. Beginning in the 1920s, umpires were also required to substitute in a new ball whenever the one in play became scuffed; prior to that, balls would be used for as long as they remained in one piece.

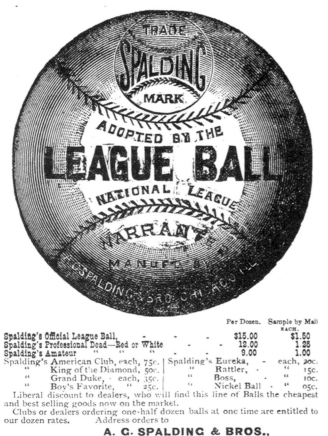

Ad for Spalding baseballs, 1882

Rawlings baseball factory, Turrialba, Costa Rica

Official ball of Major League Baseball, 2006

A new yarn that could be wound more tightly was added in 1920, and the cork center was cushioned beginning in 1926, both of which contributed to the liveliness of the baseball. The only deviation from the cork-cushioned center was during World War II, when wartime restrictions called for the use of a synthetic rubber center.

The Rawlings Sporting Goods Company took over as the official supplier to both leagues in 1976. The company produces about 750,000 balls annually for use by Major League Baseball. Each ball is hand sown with exactly 108 stitches at the Rawlings factory in Costa Rica. Both the sporting goods company and Major League Baseball insist that the materials and processes used to produce the balls has never wavered, and that any changes in home run proficiency are purely the result of human ability.

THE BAT

Aside from basic regulations about maximum length (42 inches) and maximum diameter (2 3/4 inches), the shapes and sizes of baseball bats can be as varied as the men wielding them. The lineup of bats from the National Baseball Hall of Fame in Cooperstown in the photo below gives a hint of the variation that existed over a century of baseball (from left to right): maximum length and width allowed by the rules; typical bat from the 1870s; Pete Browning's bat, 1880s; Hugh Duffy's bat, with which he compiled a .440 average in 1894; Ty Cobb's bat; Babe Ruth's bat; and Ernie Banks' bat. The earliest bats had almost no taper to the handle. The large barrel and gradually-tapering handle became the norm by the 1890s.

Pete Browning, who played for the Louisville Eclipse of the American Association from 1882 to 1889, was known for being

Al Simmons, 1931

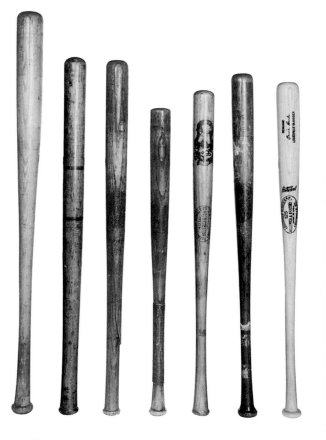

Evolution of baseball bats

particular about his bats. Legend has it that when Browning broke a favorite bat during a game in 1884, he hired woodworkers John "Bud" and J. Frederick Hillerich to produce a new one for him. In his first game with the new stick, Browning collected four hits. Other players were soon ordering custom-made bats from J. F. Hillerich and Son. Later known as Hillerich and Bradsby, the company began trademarking its bats with the Louisville Slugger brand in the 1890s. Honus Wagner, an early proponent of the Louisville Slugger, signed a contract to have his signature branded on commercially-available bats—marking the first paid endorsement of sporting goods by an athlete.

Nineteenth-century legend Wee Willie Keeler brandished one of the smallest Louisville Sluggers ever used by a major leaguer. The 140-pound Hall of Famer compiled a .341 lifetime batting average with a 30-1/2-inch bat, proving that size doesn't always matter. At the other extreme, Al Simmons' bats measured in at 38 inches and 46 ounces. The big sticks worked well for Simmons, who batted over .300 in each of his first 11 seasons in the league (1924–34). Nobody today uses a bat as heavy as Simmons'. The more common weight range is 33 to 36 ounces. Most hitters recognize that bat speed is more important that weight.

Barry Bonds, 2006

Ash, specifically northern white ash, has long been the preferred wood for bats because of its weight, strength, and durability. Hickory bats were common in the early days of baseball, but it is much heavier and is rarely if ever used today. In the late 1990s Barry Bonds helped to popularize the maple bat. Maple is heavier than ash, but it is also harder and more durable.

The cupped end is another feature of bats used by Bonds and other players. This removes weight from the bat to improve bat speed without detracting from the wood's strength. The rules state that bats have to be rounded at the end, but a cup-shaped recess, no more than one inch deep or two inches wide, is allowed. The black color of Bonds' bat is one of seven acceptable stain colors.

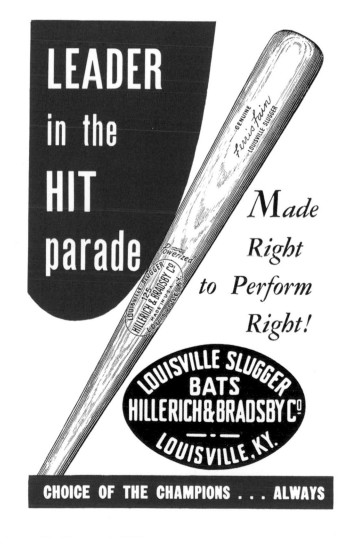

Louisville Slugger ad, 1950s

THE GLOVE

Of the sport's many advances over the last 150 years, none is more universally appreciated than the glove or mitt. Prior to the 1870s, ballplayers took the field barehanded, resulting in many bruised and broken fingers, as the sketch below from Albert Spalding's 1911 book, *America's National Game*, suggests. Charlie Waitt is credited as the first to use gloves in the field. In 1875 he donned a pair of leather gloves, but was taunted by the fans for being a "sissy." At the time, wearing gloves was seen as a sign of weakness, which is ironic considering that these early gloves were thin pieces of leather more akin to today's batting gloves than to fielding gloves. The gloves, made from horsehide or buckskin, were often worn on both hands, with the fingers cut off on the throwing hand. The palm and knuckle areas were minimally padded. The primary function of the early gloves was protection, rather than as an aid in fielding, as the glove would later become.

As a player in the late 1870s, Al Spalding was one of the first to bring legitimacy to wearing gloves in the field, and as owner of

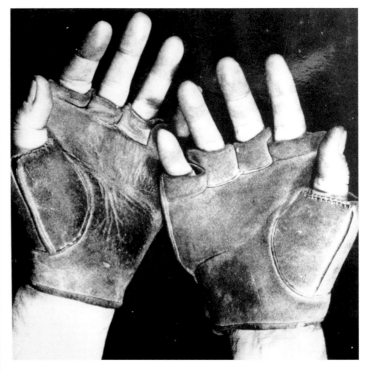

Fielder's gloves, 1870s

Sherry Magee, circa 1910

A. G. Spalding and Brothers sporting goods company, he was a pioneer in glove production for players nationwide. First gaining popularity among catchers and first basemen, gloves were widely accepted and worn at all positions by the turn of the century. Joining Spalding in the glove business were its subsidiary A. J. Reach and the Rawlings Sporting Goods Company of St. Louis.

Fielder before the days of gloves, from America's National Game

Glove style and design today varies by position and personal taste. Infielders tend to wear a smaller glove so that they can grasp the ball more easily for a quick throw to the base. Second baseman Craig Biggio's glove is barely larger than his hand, but it was big enough to help him win four-consecutive Gold Glove awards at the pivot position. Ken Griffey Jr.—who has garnered more Gold Gloves than any outfielder since Roberto Clemente and Willie Mays—uses the longer glove typical of his position. Griffey's Rawlings Trap-Eze model features the sixth finger within the webbing. Pitchers prefer gloves with an enclosed webbing in order to hide the ball as they grip it for a pitch.

Craig Biggio, 2000

Sherry Magee (shown near left), an outfielder with the Philadelphia Phillies in the early 1900s, donned the simple five-fingered, non-webbed glove typical of the era. Additional padding was provided in the palm and above the wrist.

In 1920, St. Louis pitcher Bill Doak approached Rawlings with the idea of adding web-lacing between the thumb and index finger to create a natural pocket in which to receive the ball. Doak's model remained in production for decades and provided the basis for future designs. In the 1940s, Rawlings developed and patented the "Deep Well" pocket. The Trap-Eze model, originated in the 1960s, features a finger-like extension within the webbing.

Ken Griffey Jr., 2005

CATCHER'S EQUIPMENT

Baseball is not, by definition, a contact sport—unless you happen to play catcher. Foul tips, errant pitches, and charging base runners conspire to take their toll on the catcher's hands, legs, back, neck, and other body parts. In the early days, wearing any kind of protective equipment was considered a sign of weakness, and so catchers didn't wear any, at least not visibly.

By the 1880s rule changes mandating that the third strike be caught in the air (and thus requiring the catcher to move closer to the batter) and permitting pitchers to throw overhand hastened the acceptance of equipment for the catcher. Catcher's mitts evolved from fingerless gloves, similar to what other fielders used at the time, to shapeless, pillow-like mitts consisting of a thick pad over the palm. Mitts with defined pockets were not introduced until the 1930s. The advent of flexible hinged mitts by the 1960s allowed

Sketch depicting the physical ailments of catchers, 1800s

George Gibson, circa 1908

Roger Bresnahan, circa 1910

catchers to receive the ball one-handed, and thus keep their throwing hand out of the line of fire.

Masks emerged at about the same time as the first gloves. Catchers initially wore mouth-guards, similar to what boxers wear, but in the mid-1870s Fred Thayer adapted a fencing mask for use in baseball. Subsequent improvements not only better protected the catchers' faces, but also helped to improve visibility and thus fielding.

By the end of the twentieth century, the catcher's mask had evolved from steel-and-leather cages, such the one modeled by George Gibson in 1908, to futuristic helmets made from high-tech polycarbons. These helmets, as exhibited by Washington's Brian Schneider, protect the sides and back of the head and offer better peripheral vision.

Roger Bresnahan, a Hall of Fame catcher who spent nearly 1,000 games behind the plate between 1900 and 1915, introduced another essential element to the "tools of ignorance"—as catcher's equipment is affectionately known. To protect his shins from wayward pitches and sliding, spikes-first base runners, in 1908 Bresnahan modified the leg guards worn by cricket players. He also sported an improved mask that season. From 1905 to 1907

Brian Schneider, Washington Nationals, 2006

Bresnahan caught an average of 88 games per year; in 1908 he was behind the plate for 139 games. Fiberboard eventually replaced the cane rods of Bresnahan's guards, and padded leather was extended around the knees and ankles. For today's backstops, molded plastics and firm padding provide protection from the tips of the toes to the top of the knees.

Worn under the uniform, chest protectors were a more easily concealable piece of equipment for catchers trying to assert their toughness in the 1870s and 1880s, but the pads provided only minimal cushion. More malleable, tougher stuffing was introduced early in 1900s, and it has continued to evolve with technology over the century. The basic outline has changed little since Bresnahan's day, and today's chest protectors can absorb 90-mile-per-hour fastballs or 230-pound base runners.

Ty Wigginton collides with catcher Yadier Molina, 2004

THE UNIFORM

Within a few years of forming the New York Knickerbockers as the first organized baseball club, the members of the team were wearing coordinated outfits: straw hats, white flannel shirts, and long blue pants. In the 1850s and 1860s, common uniform features included collared shirts, bibs, ties, and large belts.

By the 1870s, knickers (not, as one might think, introduced by the Knickerbockers) replaced long pants as the trouser of choice. The color of the stockings below the knickers was usually the identifying feature—thus you had teams nicknamed the White Stockings, Red Stockings, and Brown Stockings. (These teams are not, incidentally, the forebears of the White Sox, Red Sox, and Browns but rather of the Cubs, Braves, and Cardinals.) The Brown Stockings became the Cardinals when they changed their socks from brown to red. The Tigers' nickname came from the yellow-and-black striped socks worn by the Detroit club.

Brooklyn Excelsiors, 1860

Tim Murnane, Philadelphia Athletics, 1872

BASE BALL PLAYERS' SUPPLIES.

NOTE.—Clubs wishing complete outfits will be furnished with samples of first and second quality flannels, opera cloth and belt webbing on application.

REDUCED PRICES FOR 1878.
PECK & SNYDER,
Designers and Leaders of Base Ball Fashions,
124 NASSAU STREET, NEW YORK.

Uniform ad, 1878

Cy Young, Boston Americans, 1902

Uniforms were made of wool or wool-cotton blends well into the twentieth century. They tended to be loose fitting and worn in a baggy style. Jerseys with half- or three-quarter-length sleeves were worn over long- or short-sleeved t-shirts, depending on the weather. Pittsburgh and a few other clubs had the option of the detachable sleeve, buttoned at the elbow. The fold-down collar had faded out by the 1910s, when the collarless or upright military-style look came into fashion. Button-down fronts were the norm for most teams by the turn of the century, although the Boston Americans (Red Sox) retained the laced front until about 1910. The Cubs introduced the zippered front in the 1930s.

Most clubs wore white uniforms for home games and gray uniforms on the road. Some teams, such as the New York Giants, opted for solid black or dark blue road uniforms. Colored pinstripes made their debut around the turn of the century; the iconic Yankees pinstripes didn't appear until 1915. Brooklyn added horizontal stripes to their vertical pinstripes in 1916, creating a unique checkerboard

look. Colored trim along the shirtfront or on the sleeves was another embellishment to the white and gray uniforms. Big, knitted sweaters worn over the uniforms, such as the one worn by Chief Bender in 1911 in the photo below, were the predecessors of the windbreaker-style warm-up jackets that followed.

Cap styles also assumed a variety of forms. In the National League's inaugural season of 1876, Albert Spalding dressed each of his players in a different-colored hat, although that experiment was quickly abandoned. A dark-colored bill and a lighter top, sometimes with descending stripes, was a popular style in the early 1900s. The pillbox-style cap with horizontal stripes caught on with the Philadelphia Athletics and a few other teams in the 1910s—a look that was brought back into style in the 1970s by the Pittsburgh Pirates.

Howie Camnitz, Pittsburgh Pirates, 1911

Chief Meyers, New York Giants, and Chief Bender, Philadelphia Athletics, 1911

The Uniform:
Evolution of Dodgers Uniforms

Brooklyn Bridegrooms, 1889

Bill Dahlen, Brooklyn Superbas, 1910

Casey Stengel, Brooklyn Robins, 1915

Ivy Olson, Brooklyn Robins, 1916

Billy Loes, Brooklyn Dodgers, 1953

John Tudor, Los Angeles Dodgers, 1988

Brad Penny, Los Angeles Dodgers, 2006

Houston Astros, 1986

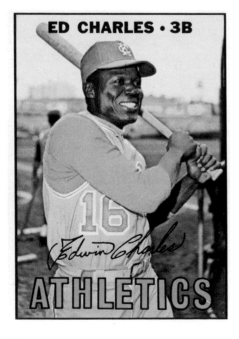

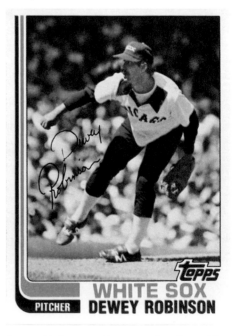

Ed Charles, Kansas City Athletics, 1967   *Rennie Stennett, Pittsburgh Pirates, 1979*   *Dewey Robinson, Chicago White Sox, 1982*

THE UNIFORM

Similar to today's retro-style ballparks, baseball uniforms by the end of the twentieth century evoked the clean, classy look of earlier eras. White and gray base colors adorned with little more than pinstripes and the team's name or logo characterize the modern uniform.

The tailored flannels of the 1960s gave way to cooler, more durable, and tighter-fitting doubleknit fabrics in the 1970s. That decade also saw an explosion of inventive colors and styles. Always the nonconformist, Athletics owner Charlie Finley was the first to break the color barrier, as it were, in baseball uniforms. His Kansas City club first took the field in combinations of green, gold, and white in 1963, and they carried the look to Oakland during the seventies.

The Houston Astros took it to an extreme with their vibrant combination of oranges, reds, and yellows. The Pittsburgh Pirates went retro with the squared pillbox hat beginning in 1976—although the bright gold uniforms were anything but old-style. In Chicago, Bill Veeck revived the fold-down collars, and he even experimented with dressing his White Sox players in short pants.

As the more staid, retro-inspired look became the trend in the 1990s, colors returned to more muted tones; pullover jerseys gave way to the button-down front; beltless trousers with wide elastic bands went by the wayside; and graphics were simplified. Although the doubleknit fabric is well-suited to stretchable, form-fitting garments, some players assumed the baggy look that was popular many decades earlier.

The sleeveless vest, a style first introduced by the Chicago Cubs in 1940, was made popular in the late-1950s and 1960s by the Cincinnati Reds and Pittsburgh Pirates, among others. Both of those teams brought it back into their wardrobes in the 1990s and early 2000s.

Through all the fashion trends, some clubs have left their uniforms virtually unchanged. The New York Yankees have maintained their distinctive pinstripes, with the NY logo on home uniforms and the city name on road uniforms, since the 1930s. The Detroit Tigers steered clear of the elastic bands and accent colors on their home uniforms throughout the 1970s and '80s. The elegant "D" has graced the left breast of Detroit players from Ty Cobb through Hank Greenberg and Alan Trammel to Magglio Ordóñez.

Ken Griffey Jr., Cincinnati Reds, and Sean Casey, Pittsburgh Pirates, 2006

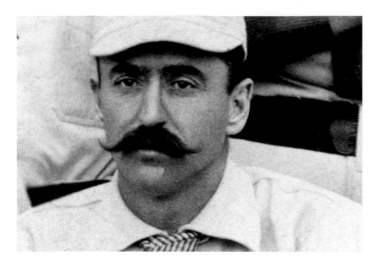

Ned Hanlon, 1889

Frenchy Bordagaray, 1936

GROOMING

Sideburns, muttonchops, handlebars—facial hair took many wild forms back in the seventies . . . the 1870s. Mustaches and other embellishments were common among nineteenth-century ballplayers. Ned Hanlon had a Hall of Fame managerial career from 1889 to 1907, and in his first year as player-manager of the Pittsburgh Alleghenys, he sported a classic handlebar mustache.

Throughout much of the twentieth century, teams had strict rules against growing facial hair of any kind. One maverick in this regard was Stanley "Frenchy" Bordagaray. In 1936 the eccentric outfielder for the Brooklyn Dodgers arrived at Spring Training sporting a mustache, which he had grown for a movie role in the offseason. Bordagaray soon added a goatee to his look. Although Brooklyn's manager, Casey Stengel, was known as a free-thinker himself, Frenchy was told to shave after an early-season slump. He finished the season with a .315 batting average, the best of his career.

As the counterculture infiltrated mainstream America in the 1960s, baseball retained its clean-cut image, until Oakland A's owner Charlie Finley challenged the league standards once again. Finley offered each member of his team $500 to grow a mustache by Father's Day in 1972, when the team would host a Mustache Day promotion at the ballpark. Every player showed up mustachioed and earned their bonus. Rollie Fingers met the assignment most creatively with his distinctive handlebar.

As the mustachioed look infiltrated even the conservative realm of George Steinbrenner's Yankees, free-spirited hair styles were on full display. A number of African American players grew their Afros out during the decade.

Jim Bunning, circa 1962

Thirty years later, certain hair styles have come full circle. The Boston Red Sox, proudly christening themselves "the Idiots," grew out their hair and went unshaven during their championship run in 2004. Center fielder Johnny Damon had to crop his flowing mane, however, when he signed with the rival Yankees in 2006.

Rollie Fingers, 1973

Oscar Gamble, 1975

Johnny Damon, 2005

Johnny Damon, 2006

Knickerbocker and Excelsior baseball clubs, circa 1858

LEAGUES AND TEAMS

Baseball in the mid-nineteenth century was played mostly by loosely organized groups of amateurs. The Knickerbocker Base Ball Club of New York formed as the first organized amateur team in 1845. Over the next decade the Knicks were joined by the Atlantics, Excelsiors, and others around the region. In 1857, 16 clubs from New York and Brooklyn assembled at the first annual Base Ball Convention. By 1866 more than 200 clubs from around the country attended the convention.

In 1876, the National League of Professional Base Ball Players was established as the sport's organizing body. Over the next 25 years, the league survived considerable franchise turnover, player-looting, rampant gambling, on-field brawls, and competing leagues. In 1892 it absorbed four clubs from the rival American Association and operated as a 12-team league before returning to eight teams in 1900.

When the American League established itself as a bonafide major league at the turn of the century, it went head-to-head with the National League, competing for players and fans. Peace was achieved within a couple of years, however, and the two

National League clubs, 1895

leagues survived with the same 16 franchises in the same cities for half a century.

Teams began to get restless by the middle of the twentieth century. Between 1953 and 1957 five of the major leagues' 16 franchises relocated. Boston lost the Braves to Milwaukee, the Browns left St.

Louis to become the Baltimore Orioles, the Philadelphia Athletics headed to Kansas City, and New Yorkers watched as the Giants and Dodgers picked up and moved to California. Milwaukee fans eagerly welcomed their first taste of the big leagues since the American League's original Milwaukee club moved to St. Louis in 1902. Attendance at Milwaukee County Stadium surpassed two million in 1954, the team's second year in the new city; the Braves had drawn a total of 281,278 fans in their final season in Boston.

The complexion of Major League Baseball continued to change in the 1960s. The American League expanded by two teams in 1961, and in 1962 the National League added the New York Mets and the Houston Colt .45s (as they were known before becoming the Astros in 1965). By 1969, the number of clubs increased to 24. The leagues each split into two six-team divisions in 1969, and the postseason was expanded to include a League Championship Series between division winners. Also in 1969, baseball crossed the border with the birth of the Montreal Expos.

Milwaukee Braves program, 1954

Canada got a second team in 1976 when the Toronto Blue Jays (along with the Seattle Mariners) came on board, increasing the total number of teams to 26.

Since 1994 each league has been composed of three divisions, and a wildcard team has figured in the postseason picture. Where teams previously had to win only four out of seven (and for a brief period five out of nine) World Series games to claim the title of "world champions," they now have to win 11 out of a possible 19 postseason games. All this after a regular-season schedule that increased from 154 games to 162 games in 1962.

When the Expos moved to Washington, D.C., in 2004—the first franchise to relocate since the Senators moved to Texas in 1972—the makeup of today's Major League Baseball was in place. From a low of six National League clubs in 1877 and 1878, the majors have expanded to 30 teams in 27 cities.

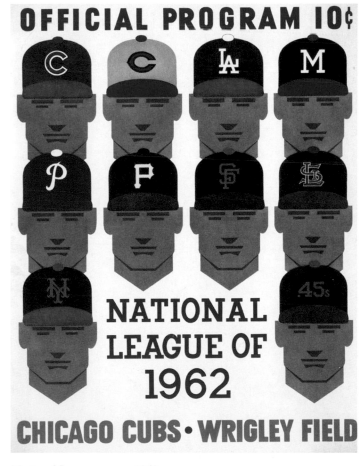

National League teams, 1962

THE RACE BARRIER

The exclusion of African American players from professional baseball was perpetuated by informal agreement among teams throughout the nineteenth century. A number of all-black amateur teams did occasionally compete against white teams in exhibition matches, and some semipro or minor league clubs had integrated squads. The team portrait of the Keokuk Westerns from 1885 shows a lone black player, Bud Fowler, among his all-white teammates.

Moses Fleetwood Walker was a catcher for the semipro Toledo Mudhens in 1883. When Toledo joined the American Association in 1884, Walker became the first black player in a major league. While playing for the Newark Little Giants of the International League, Walker and pitcher George Stovey formed the first all-black battery in organized ball. After Cap Anson's Chicago White Stockings refused to play an exhibition game against Newark in 1887, the International League owners voted to not sign any more black players. By 1897, the National League and most of the minor leagues had followed suit. The prohibition against African Americans never formally entered the rule book, but segregation in baseball remained an unofficial yet firmly enforced "gentleman's agreement" for another 50 years.

With most of organized baseball shut off to them, African American ballplayers continued to form their own teams in the late 1800s. Rube Foster was a driving force behind organizing a league of black teams after the turn of the century. In 1920, he brought together teams from Chicago, Dayton, Detroit, Indianapolis, Kansas City, and New York to form the Negro National League.

Keokuk Westerns, 1885

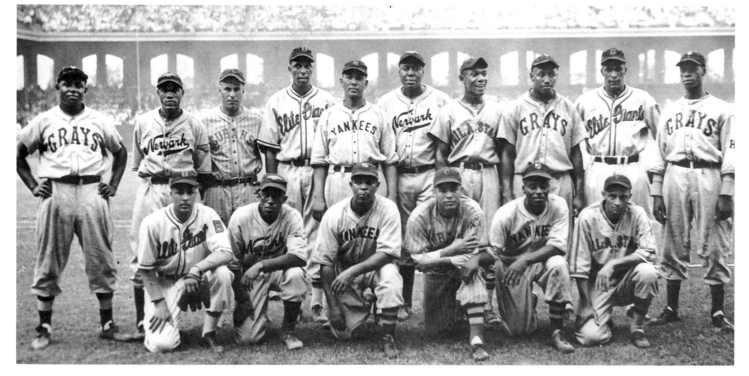

Negro Leagues East-West All-Star Game, 1939

Brooklyn Dodgers, 1947

Other all-black leagues also took shape during the 1920s and 1930s. The Negro National League disbanded in 1931 but a new incarnation was revived two years later. The league instituted an annual East-West All-Star Game, played at Chicago's Comiskey Park, to showcase the talents of ballplayers like Buck Leonard, Josh Gibson, Oscar Charleston, Judy Johnson, Martin Dihigo, and Satchel Paige, among many others.

When Jackie Robinson broke baseball's color line and joined the Brooklyn Dodgers in 1947, he was the sole African American in the game. Over the next few years, future Hall of Famers such as Larry Doby, Roy Campanella, Willie Mays, Ernie Banks, and Hank Aaron made the leap from the Negro Leagues to the majors. The Boston Red Sox were the last major league team to integrate when they signed Pumpsie Green in 1959.

The percentage of major league ballplayers today who are African American is lower than it was in the 1970s, but a few teams have African American mangers. Frank Robinson was the first, when he was named player-manager of the Cleveland Indians in 1975. In 2002, when Robinson was managing the Montreal Expos, he was one of six black skippers in Major League Baseball, along with Hal McRae of the Tampa Bay Devil Rays, Dusty Baker of the San Francisco Giants, Lloyd McClendon of the Pittsburgh Pirates, Jerry Royster of the Milwaukee Brewers, and Don Baylor of the Chicago Cubs. In 2005, Willie Randolph of the Mets became the first black manager of a New York team.

Frank Robinson and Willie Randolph, 2005

FROM NATIONAL PASTIME TO INTERNATIONAL PASTIME

From the birth of organized ball in the mid-1800s until the second half of the twentieth century, the participants at the major league level were almost exclusively white, native-English speakers. Some immigrants did join up with teams in the late-nineteenth century, but they were mostly from England, Scotland, and Ireland. The first Latin American to play organized ball in the United States was Esteban "Steve" Bellán. Born in Havana, Cuba, Bellán came to this country as a student and went to play for the Union Base Ball Club of Lansingburgh, New York, in 1868. (The team later became the Troy Haymakers of the National Association.) Typical of the local orientation of teams of the period, all of Bellán's teammates were natives of either New York or Pennsylvania.

Cuba was the main source of Latino players in the majors until the 1960s. The first major leaguer from the Dominican Republic was Ozzie Virgil Sr., who joined the New York Giants in 1956. Since then, more than 400 Dominicans have played in the majors—by far the largest contingent of foreigners in Major League Baseball. In 1999, President Leonel Fernandez of the Dominican Republic joined Hall of Famer Juan Marichal and nine Dominican players from the Cardinals and Cubs in a pre-game ceremony at Busch Stadium to honor that nation's contributions to the sport.

On the other side of the globe, baseball was introduced to Japan by American traders in the late-nineteenth century. American all-star teams embarked on exhibition tours of the country as early as 1908. The 1934 tour squad included Babe Ruth and Lou Gehrig, among other baseball greats. Ruth—and his 13 home runs in 18 games—did as much as anything to carry the sport to new heights of popularity.

With professional leagues now thriving in Japan as well as Taiwan and South Korea, the number of Asian-born players in the United States is also steadily on the rise. Pitcher Hideo Nomo joined the Dodgers in 1995 and was the first Japanese native to have a significant career in the States. Today, more than two dozen Asian players play in the majors. The Los Angeles Dodgers' 2006 squad featured Takashi Saito of Japan, Jae Weong Seo of

Union Base Ball Club of Lansingburgh, 1869

Babe Ruth and bat boys, Koshien Stadium, Osaka, Japan, 1934

South Korea, and Hong-Chih Kuo of Taiwan on the pitching staff alone.

In 2006, every major league team included at least one foreign-born player on its roster. The New York Mets featured the highest number of foreign-born players (15). The 2006 Dodgers had players from 10 different nations (United States, Canada, Mexico, Panama, Cuba, Dominican Republic, Venezuela, Japan, South Korea, and Taiwan) and one U.S. commonwealth (Puerto Rico).

Dominican baseball players with President Leonel Fernandez, 1999

Above: Takashi Saito and Jae Seo, 2006

Left: Hideo Nomo, 1995

Baltimore Orioles, 1896

Mike Donlin, 1905

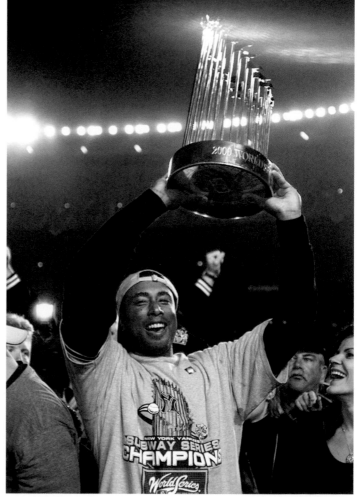

Bernie Williams, 2000

DYNASTIES

In the 1800s, league championships went to the team with the best regular-season record. Harry Wright's Boston Red Stockings won four such titles during the National Association's five seasons, and the Boston club continued to dominate after shifting to the National League. Known as the Red Caps (1876–82) and the Beaneaters (1883–1906), they won eight titles in the league's first quarter-century. The club masterminded so-called small-ball in the 1890s with such tactics as the sacrifice bunt, the hit-and-run, and the stolen base. Boston's main rival during the decade was the Baltimore Orioles. Baltimore perpetuated small-ball and added a dimension of intimidation and, by some accounts, outright cheating. Led by manger Ned Hanlon and featuring Hall of Famers Willie Keeler, Hughie Jennings, and John McGraw, Baltimore won three-straight titles from 1894 to 1896. The Chicago White Stockings (later the Cubs) laid claim to six of the NL's first 11 crowns. Among them, Boston, Chicago, and Baltimore grabbed all but eight of the league's championship banners prior to 1901.

The reign of the few continued in the new century. Every National League pennant from 1901 to 1913 was won by the Pittsburgh Pirates (four), Chicago Cubs (four), or New York Giants (five). The Giants, under manager John McGraw, won a total of 10 league pennants in the first 25 years of the century. Outfielder Mike Donlin was New York's top hitter during the first championship season in 1905.

Of course, the story of baseball dynasties belongs to another New York franchise: the Yankees. From 1921 through 2003 the Yanks won 38 American League pennants and 26 world championships—more than twice as many as any other franchise. The apex of Yankees dominance may have been the period from 1936 to 1943, when the Bronx Bombers won seven pennants and six World Series in eight years. Or, it may have been the 12 seasons under manager Casey Stengel (1949–60), when they won seven crowns and missed the World Series only twice.

Since the advent of divisional play in 1969 and free agency in the mid-1970s, dynasties have been harder to come by. The

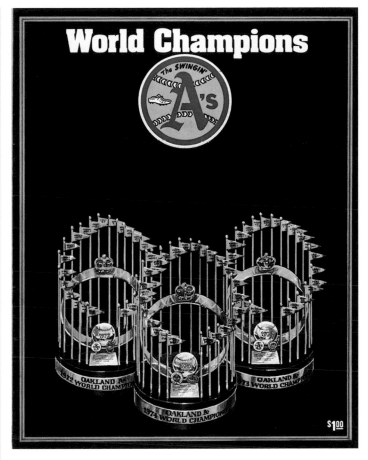

Oakland A's championship trophies, 1972–74

Oakland A's were the only team to win more than three World Series between 1969 and 1999: three in a row from 1972 to 1974 and a fourth 15 years later, in 1989. During the 1980s, nine different franchises won a championship—the only decade in which that has happened.

The Yankees returned as a dynastic force around the turn of the twenty-first century. Under manager Joe Torre, the men in pinstripes won six pennants from 1996 to 2003. In the photo on the facing page, Bernie Williams hoists the team's third-straight World Championship trophy after defeating the New York Mets in the 2000 World Series.

Game One, 1903 World Series, Huntington Avenue Grounds

THE WORLD SERIES

Beginning in 1894, the National League experimented with an exhibition championship series between the league's top two finishers from the regular season. The winner was to receive the Temple Cup. The Baltimore Orioles reached the series four years in a row, and won two of them, but player and fan interest quickly waned. The last Temple Cup series was played in 1897.

In 1903, the American League and National League owners agreed to put their rivalry aside and organize a postseason series between the winners of the two leagues. Late in the season, with his team comfortably in first place, Pittsburgh Pirates owner Barney Dreyfuss contacted Henry Killea, owner of the AL-leading Boston Americans, and the two men laid the plans for a best-of-nine series to determine the "World's Championship" of baseball. On

October 1, 1903, the Americans and Pirates faced off at Boston's Huntington Avenue Grounds before a capacity crowd of 16,242. Eager fans poured onto the field as the teams began their pre-game warm-ups, and police had to drive them back to the outfield before the game could begin. Although only 7,455 fans turned out for the eighth game on October 13, Boston secured its fifth win of the series to clinch victory in baseball's inaugural World Series. The final game was completed in a mere one hour and thirty-five minutes. For their efforts, each member of the Boston squad received a $1,182 share of the receipts. Just over 100,000 fans attended the eight games.

Over the next 102 years, through 2005, the World Series has been played in front of more than 26.8 million attendees. In 1959, when half the games were played at Los Angeles' mammoth Memorial Coliseum, more than 420,000 people attended the six-game series; a record 92,706 witnessed Game Five in Los Angeles.

The Chicago White Sox were the losers in that 1959 series, but in 2005 the ChiSox found redemption after an 88-year championship drought. In a four-game sweep of the Houston Astros, the series drew 42,106 fans per game. Every game was played at night (as has been the case since 1985), and they lasted an average of three hours and fifty-one minutes, a World Series record. When the White Sox won their last title in 1917, the players earned a $3,669 share; the 2005 White Sox earned approximately $325,000 apiece from the postseason receipts. The losing Astros walked away with just shy of $192,000 per man.

Game Five, 1959 World Series, Los Angeles Memorial Coliseum

Game One, 2005 World Series, U.S. Cellular Field

THE ALL-STAR GAME

Above: 1933 National League All-Stars

Below: 1933 American League All-Stars

E xhibition matches involving the game's top stars is a tradition that goes back to the nineteenth century. In 1858 the all-stars from New York faced off against the best from Brooklyn in a three-game series that attracted capacity crowds at Long Island's Fashion Race Course.

The annual All-Star Game between the best from the American and National Leagues began in 1933. The game was proposed by Arch Ward, sports editor for the Chicago *Tribune*, as an exhibition to coincide with the city's Century of Progress Exposition. The first modern All-Star Game was played in front of 49,200 fans at Comiskey Park on July 6, 1933. John McGraw, who came out of retirement, and Connie Mack were named the managers of the all-star squads, and fans voted for the players. The game featured 20 future Hall of Famers, including Frankie Frisch, Carl Hubbell, and Paul Waner from the National League and Jimmie Foxx, Lou

SHARKEY, CONROY, GEHRIG, RUTH, HILDEBRAND, MACK, CRONIN, GROVE, SHARKEY, DICKEY, SIMMONS, GOMEZ, WES FERRELL, DYKES, SHARKEY, SCHACHT, COLLINS, LAZZERI, CROWDER, FOXX, FLETCHER, AVERILL, ROMMEL, CHAPMAN, FERRELL, WEST, GEHRINGER, MCBRIDE

AMERICAN LEAGUE ALL-STAR GAME

1933

Gehrig, Lefty Grove, and Babe Ruth from the American League. The 38-year-old Ruth came through with a two-run homer in the third inning, which proved the difference in the American League's 4-2 victory.

For most of All-Star Game history, the starters have been selected by the fans. One exception was the period from 1935 to 1946, when the managers picked the rosters. Voting returned to the fans in 1947, but after Cincinnati supporters stuffed the ballot boxes with votes for the Reds players in 1958, the selection shifted to the managers, coaches, and players. Since 1970 it has been the people's privilege once again. Fans vote for the 16 starters, and pitchers and reserves are chosen by the managers. As of 2005, the fans also vote for the final roster spots after the first 31 players on each team are announced. In addition to ballots at ballparks around the league, All-Star votes can be cast from all over the world through Major League Baseball's website. Sixteen million ballots were cast in 2005.

In 2003, the All-Star Game was given added significance by granting home-field advantage in the World Series to the league

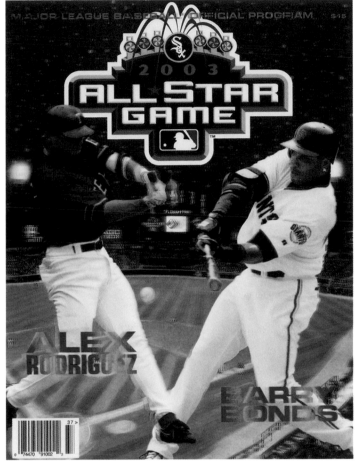

2003 All-Star Game program

Alfonso Soriano and Albert Pujols, 2003 All-Star Game

that wins the All-Star Game. The first game under this rule was played at Chicago's U.S. Cellular Field. All-Star Weekend 2003 featured a full slate of events, including the All-Star Legends and Celebrity Softball Game; the All-Star Futures Game, featuring top prospects from the minor leagues; and the Home Run Derby—all of which carry corporate-sponsored names. The main event in 2003 drew 47,609 fans, and millions more watched on television around the globe. The American League won the game 7-6—but the AL-champion Yankees lost to the Florida Marlins in the World Series despite having home-field advantage.

THE HOME RUN

During baseball's dead-ball era, prior to 1920, long home runs simply were not a significant part of the game. One notable exception was the 1884 season in Chicago. For that one season, balls hit over the fences at Lakefront Park—a mere 180 feet to left field and 196 feet to right—were ruled home runs; in other years they were ground-rule doubles. As a result, the Chicago White Stockings knocked 142 home runs in 1884, 129 more than they had the previous season. The entire rest of the league hit only 180 homers combined in 1884. Ned Williamson led Chicago with 27, nearly doubling the previous single-season record of 14 set a year earlier by Harry Stovey. The original ground rules were reinstated at Lakefront Park in 1885, but Williamson's record was in the books, where it stood for 35 years.

In 1919, Boston's Babe Ruth switched from being a pitcher to an outfielder with a regular spot in the lineup—and baseball was changed forever. That year, Ruth hit 29 home runs. After he was traded to New York in 1920, he shattered his own record with 54 homers, out-homering every other American League *team*. In 1921, he set another new mark at 59. Ruth's 60 home runs in 1927 was the high-water mark in the major leagues for more than three decades.

Before Ruth arrived in New York in 1920, only five players had ever hit 20 home runs in a season; Ruth alone hit 20 or more in 16-consecutive seasons. He hit 50 or more four times. Following Ruth's retirement in 1935, the 50-homer level was reached only a dozen times in the next 60 seasons, including Roger Maris' record-setting 61 in 1961.

The period since 1995 has seen unprecedented home run production. From 1995 to 2005, players hit more than 50 homers in a

RUTH HITS 60TH HOME RUN

Babe Ruth, 1921

season 19 times. In the first 129 years of professional baseball, only two men hit 60 or more home runs in a season. Three players accomplished the feat a total of six times from 1998 to 2001; Sammy Sosa *averaged* more than 60 during that span. Mark McGwire and Barry Bonds each hit over 70 home runs.

In 2000, 5,693 home runs were belted, for an average of 1.17 per game. In the peak season during Ruth's career, 1930, the league average was 0.63 home runs per game. Juiced or not, players have hit a lot of baseballs out of the ballpark in the last decade.

Chicago White Stockings, 1885

Barry Bonds, 1998

Sammy Sosa, 2001

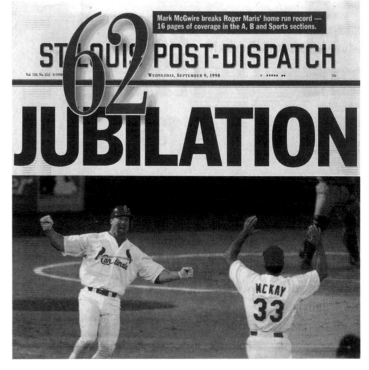

THE ALL-TIME HOME RUN KINGS

Harry Stovey finished among the top 10 in home runs 11 times in his 14-year career. He led the league five times. When he retired in 1893, Stovey had more home runs than anybody else ever to play the game. Harry Stovey hit a total 122 lifetime home runs.

Babe Ruth had Stovey beat by his fourth season as an outfielder. In 1923, Ruth became the first player to break the 200-homer

Babe Ruth and Jimmie Foxx, 1930s

plateau. He would go on to be the first to reach 300 career home runs, the first to 400, the first to 500, the first to 600, and the first to 700. His 714 lifetime long-balls stood as the record for nearly 40 years. (Stovey had been surpassed by Roger Connor as the home run king two years after he retired.)

By the time of Ruth's death in 1948, only two other men had joined him in the elite 500-homer club: Jimmie Foxx (534) and Mel Ott (511). During the 1950s, eight players entered the majors who would go on to knock more than 500 dingers in their careers. One would break 700.

When Ruth hit his 137th career homer to pass Roger Connor as home run king in July of 1921, not much attention was paid in the media or by the fans. It was a different story half a century later when Hank Aaron made his run at the immortal Babe. Aaron,

Harry Stovey tobacco card, 1888

Barry Bonds, 2006

Hank Aaron, 1974

who ended the 1973 season with 713 home runs, received nearly a million pieces of mail that year—some supportive, some violently hostile. Hundreds of reporters were on hand in Cincinnati for Aaron's first game in 1974. "Hammerin' Hank" didn't wait long and knocked number 714 on his first swing of the bat. Four days later, in front of 53,775 fans at the Braves' home opener, Aaron passed Ruth to assume the throne.

When Hank Aaron retired in 1976 with 755 career home runs, 10 other players in the history of the game had as many as 500. Thirty years later, the 500-homer club has 20 members. Between 1999 and 2004, Mark McGwire, Barry Bonds, Sammy Sosa, Rafael Palmeiro, and Ken Griffey Jr.—all players who debuted in the majors in 1986 or 1989—belted number 500.

Although the accomplishments of McGwire, Bonds, Sosa, and Palmeiro have been sullied by the steroid controversy, America's fascination with the long ball remains as strong as ever. As Bonds approached and then passed Ruth for the number-two spot on the all-time list early in 2006, it was the top sports story for weeks—even when he went homerless, it was a story. Televised games were interrupted to show Bonds at bat, just in case he hit the big one. Although Bonds didn't receive the racial threats that were heaped on Aaron, he earned ample taunting and derision for the steroid rumors swirling around him.

Above: Babe Ruth and Lou Gehrig, 1920s

Right: Roger Maris at bat with Mickey Mantle on deck, 1960

DYNAMIC DUOS

With nine players on each side, baseball is a game that requires a team effort. For all of Babe Ruth's greatness and home run prowess, he was not, of course, a one-man show. Ruth's Hall of Fame teammate, Lou Gehrig, was arguably the second-best player in the American League at the time, and the pair formed one of the greatest tandems in sports history. This dynamic duo finished first and second in home runs in five-consecutive seasons (1927–31). They were the top two in on-base plus slugging percentage (OPS) in four of those seasons. Ruth was first and Gehrig second in runs scored three years in a row (1926–28). Between Gehrig's arrival in 1925 and Ruth's departure a decade later, the Yankees won three World Series.

After Ruth and Gehrig, only one other pair of teammates has finished in the top two on the home run leaderboard more than once, and it was another pinstriped duo. The M&M Boys, Mickey Mantle and Roger Maris, battled each other for the AL home run crown in 1960 and 1961. In their first season as teammates, Mantle led the league with 40 while Maris fell just short with 39. Maris' 61 homers a year later outpaced Mantle by seven as they both chased Ruth's single-season record in 1961.

The record for home runs by teammates over a career belongs to Hank Aaron and Eddie Mathews, who played together in Milwaukee and Atlanta from 1954 to 1966. They combined for 863 homers with the Braves. Because players switch teams so frequently in the free-agent era, it seems unlikely that Aaron and Mathews' record will be challenged. Ken Griffey Jr. and Alex Rodriguez hit 414 homers in less than five years as teammates on the Seattle Mariners before Griffey departed for Cincinnati after the 1999 season.

Manny Ramirez and David Ortiz, 2005

The fun-loving combination of Manny Ramirez and David Ortiz helped to carry the Boston Red Sox to a World Championship in 2003. In 2004, Ramirez led the AL with 43 homers while Ortiz finished in a tie for second with 41. They combined to hit 90 home runs in 2005, but finished second and third behind Rodriguez for the league lead. More than an all-star duo on the field, Ortiz and Ramirez are close off the field as well—something that was not always the case with Ruth and Gehrig.

.400

As the number of home runs hit and runs scored approaches new heights and fans debate whether the game has become too dominated by offense, one hitting benchmark remains elusive: the .400 season. Prior to 1900, players posted batting averages better than .400 roughly 30 times (depending on which scoring system you follow). Seven players hit .400 in the American Association in 1887 alone, when walks were counted as base hits. In the National League, Philadelphia's Ed Delahanty batted above .400 three times in six seasons. Perhaps even more remarkably, Delahanty won only one

Rogers Hornsby, 1921

Copyrighted, 1895, and published by   Geo. D. Ide, 17 Exchange Place, Boston.

HUGH DUFFY,
CENTRE FIELDER OF BOSTON BASE BALL CLUB,
AND
CHAMPION BATSMAN OF THE WORLD.

Hugh Duffy, 1895

batting title (.410 in 1899). His .407 average in 1894 was only good enough for fourth best in the league—and third best on his own team! Five players hit .400 or better that season, led by Boston's Hugh Duffy at .440.

In the first 30 years of the twentieth century, hitters topped .400 a dozen times. Nap Lajoie's .426 in 1901 is the highest post-1900. Ty Cobb and Rogers Hornsby each broke the .400 milestone three times. When Bill Terry hit .401 in 1930, it marked the end of an era. Only one player since then has stroked the magical .400. Ted Williams' .406 average in 1941 was secured when he went six-for-

Rod Carew, 1980s

Tony Gwynn, 1990s

eight at the plate in a doubleheader on the final day of the season.

Since Williams retired in 1960, only three players have come within 20 points of .400. Rod Carew was a likely candidate for .400 due to his combination of speed and precise hitting. In 1977, while playing for the Minnesota Twins, he mounted his best effort. After batting .486 in the month of June, Carew slumped in July and August. A late-season surge brought him to .388, but in the end, he fell eight hits short.

Three years later, a 30-game hitting streak spurred Kansas City's George Brett to .407 in late August of 1980. The media pressure and an injured wrist slowed Brett in the final month of the season, and he ended the year at .390.

Tony Gwynn was perhaps the best pure hitter since Williams. Gwynn never batted below .300 in 19 full seasons with the San Diego Padres, and his eight batting crowns tie him with Honus Wagner for the most ever by a National Leaguer. Gwynn's peak season was 1994. Just as he was hitting his stride—he batted .475 during the month of August—the players' strike brought the season to an abrupt end with Gwynn's average sitting at .394. It was the highest average in the majors since Williams' .406 in 1941, but Gwynn came three hits shy from reaching that elusive .400.

Ty Cobb, 1914

Pete Rose career hit number 4,192, 1985

HIT MEN

Throughout history, many baseball records have been branded as "unbreakable." To be sure, Hugh Duffy's .440 batting average from 1894 is unlikely to be challenged, and Cy Young's 511 career wins are pretty safe. Others, once seemingly untouchable, inevitably fall.

Ty Cobb was undeniably the dominant hitter of the early-twentieth century. He collected at least 200 hits in a season nine times and won 11 batting titles. Cobb's .366 career average remains the highest of all-time, eight decades after his retirement. When Cobb left the game in 1928 with 4,191 career hits (the total was later corrected to 4,189), the player closest on the list trailed by nearly 700 hits—Tris Speaker, with 3,514.

Pete Rose burst onto the scene in 1963 showing the same competitive fire that served Cobb so well during his legendary career. Rose was also a pure hitter like Cobb. In Rose's third season, he led the league with 209 hits. He mounted four more 200-hit campaigns over the next five years. He was halfway to 3,000 hits after only eight seasons in the league. As Rose continued to rack up the hits, including a career-high 230 in 1973, Cobb's record seemed within reach. Rose had 2,000 hits by the time he was 32. Hit number 3,000 came in 1978, when he was 37 years old. In 1979, Rose posted his record 10th 200-hit season. Finally, at the age of 44, Pete Rose became the all-time hit leader in 1985 when he singled against San Diego's Eric Show for number 4,192.

No active player in 2006 has 3,000 hits. The closest to the milestone, Craig Biggio and Barry Bonds, are in the waning years of their careers. Pete Rose's total of 4,256 hits is not untouchable, but few contenders have emerged. Seattle's Ichiro Suzuki averaged 226 hits in his first five seasons, but he didn't get started in the major leagues until he was 27 years old. If anybody, Derek Jeter may have the best shot among current players. Jeter, whose clean-cut image could not be further from that of Cobb and Rose, collected his 2,000th career hit in May of 2006, one month shy of his 32nd

Derek Jeter, 2001

birthday. He has had four 200-hit seasons in his first 11 years in the league. Jeter would need to average 200 hits per season until he is 42 years old to reach 4,000. And he would still be 256 hits short of the record.

Ty Cobb held the record for career hits for 62 years. Lou Gehrig was baseball's top "iron man" for 56 seasons before Cal Ripken Jr. surpassed his streak of 2,130-consecutive games. Hank Aaron claimed the home run crown after Babe Ruth wore it for just 53 years. While the numbers 4,191, 2,130, and 714 carry almost iconic status for many fans of baseball history, the number 257—George Sisler's mark for base hits in a season—stood in the record books for far longer.

Sisler, who spent most of his 15-year career playing for the hapless St. Louis Browns, played in the same era as Cobb and Ruth, and although he twice batted over .400, Sisler was often caught in the shadows of those legendary figures. When Ichiro Suzuki made a run at the single-season hit record in 2004, some modern fans had never even heard of George Sisler. Yet until that year, no other player had ever amassed as many as 257 hits in a season, as Sisler did in 1920.

Ichiro Suzuki arrived in the United States in 2001 and was an immediate sensation. He had been a baseball superstar in Japan, and his impact on Major League Baseball was immediate. Playing for the Seattle Mariners, he led the American League in hits (242), stolen bases (56), and batting average (.350) in his debut season. He became only the second player in history (after Fred Lynn in 1975) to win the Rookie of the Year and Most Valuable Player awards in the same season; like Lynn, Ichiro also won a Gold Glove. Ichiro's hit totals dropped to 208 and 212 in the next two seasons, but he went on a tear in 2004. On October 1, he singled three times against the Texas Rangers to tie and then break Sisler's storied record. Ichiro ended the year with 262 hits to go along with his league-best .372 average.

Facing page: George Sisler, circa 1920   *Above: Ichiro Suzuki, 2004*

THE GREATEST OF ALL-TIME

Every generation likes to claim that the stars of its era are the best of all-time. To be sure, the ranking of the "greatest ever" is a constant debate among casual fans and experts alike. In 1914, Clark Griffith, then manager of the Washington Senators and formerly one of the top pitchers of his day, offered his view of baseball's all-time greats, based on his two decades in the game:

Clark Griffith's All-Time Team (1914)	
Catcher	Buck Ewing
First Base	Charles Comiskey
Second Base	Eddie Collins
Shortstop	Herman Long
Third Base	Jimmie Collins
Left Field	Bill Lange
Center Field	Tris Speaker
Right Field	Ty Cobb
Pitcher	Amos Rusie, Cy Young, Christy Mathewson, Walter Johnson

A decade later, Hall of Fame manager John McGraw, one of the best baseball minds of his era, compiled his selection of the greatest players in his autobiography, *My Thirty Years in the Game*. McGraw only considered players who played after 1890, when he got his start in baseball.

John McGraw's All-Time Team (1923)	
Catcher	Buck Ewing, Roger Bresnahan, Ray Schalk, Lou Criger
First Base	George Sisler, Frank Chance
Second Base	Eddie Collins, Nap Lajoie, Rogers Hornsby
Shortstop	Honus Wagner, George Davis
Third Base	Jimmie Collins
Left Field	Hugh Duffy, Ed Delahanty
Center Field	Ty Cobb, Tris Speaker
Right Field	Willie Keeler, Joe Kelley, Harry Hooper, Babe Ruth
Pitcher	Charles Bender, John Clarkson, Walter Johnson, Addie Joss, Christy Mathewson, Sadie McMahon, Nap Rucker, Amos Rusie, Rube Waddell, Ed Walsh

Ty Cobb and Honus Wagner, 1911

Ty Cobb appeared on more lists of the "greatest" than any player of his or previous eras. Honus Wagner was Cobb's top contemporary in the National League. A century after these two stars entered the league, such esteemed sources as *The Sporting News*, the Society for American Baseball Research (SABR), and the Associated Press still rank Cobb and Wagner among the top men ever to play the game.

The average fan today probably hasn't heard of many of the players named by Griffith and McGraw, especially those from the nineteenth century. Among those who had careers in the twentieth-century, Cobb, Hornsby, Johnson, Ruth, Young, Wagner, and Mathewson appeared on the MasterCard All-Century Team selected by fans and Major League Baseball in 1999. (Wagner and Mathewson were added later by a special panel.)

Albert Pujols and Barry Bonds, 2006

The All-Century Team (1999)

Catcher	Johnny Bench, Yogi Berra
First Base	Lou Gehrig, Mark McGwire
Second Base	Jackie Robinson, Rogers Hornsby
Shortstop	Cal Ripken Jr., Ernie Banks, Honus Wagner
Third Base	Mike Schmidt, Brooks Robinson
Left Field	Ted Williams, Stan Musial
Center Field	Willie Mays, Joe DiMaggio, Mickey Mantle, Ty Cobb, Ken Griffey Jr.
Right Field	Babe Ruth, Hank Aaron, Pete Rose
Pitcher	Nolan Ryan, Sandy Koufax, Cy Young, Roger Clemens, Bob Gibson, Walter Johnson, Warren Spahn, Christy Mathewson, Lefty Grove

Comparing players from different eras is always a tricky business, but the age of performance-enhancing drugs has particularly muddied the waters when contemplating where today's players rank. After Barry Bonds set a new single-season home run record in 2001 and seemed poised to make a run at Hank Aaron's all-time mark, many wondered if the seven-time MVP was worthy of the label "greatest of all-time." As allegations of steroid use mount, some now question whether Bonds is even worthy of the Hall of Fame.

Who will be on the list of the greatest of the *next* century? Most experts agree, Alex Rodriguez and Albert Pujols are likely candidates.

Surviving members of the Major League Baseball All-Century Team, 1999 World Series

Roy Campanella, 1955

Buck Ewing tobacco card, 1888

THE CATCHER

atching is generally regarded as the most difficult position on the baseball diamond. Not only is the catcher subjected to regular physical abuse, but the position also requires strategic savvy and leadership qualities in pitch selection and working with the pitching staff.

An early standout at the backstop position, and the first catcher elected to the Hall of Fame, was Buck Ewing. Active from 1880 to 1897, Ewing was known for his strong throwing arm, his versatility, and his hustle. In addition to his .303 career average, Ewing led the National League in home runs in 1883 and in triples a year later. He is the only catcher ever to collect more than 150 triples in a career. Ewing's 354 stolen bases also rank highest among players whose primary position was catcher.

Gabby Hartnett of the Chicago Cubs was the first catcher to slug more than 30 homers in a season when he hit 37 in 1930. By the 1950s, catchers were viewed more as a power position at the plate. A three-time MVP, Roy Campanella posted four 30-homer seasons between 1950 and 1955. His high mark of 41 in 1953 stood as a record among catchers until 1996. Yogi Berra, also a three-time MVP in the fifties, was the first catcher to break the 300-career-homer plateau. Meanwhile, Yogi and Campy combined to steal a total of 55 bases in their entire major league careers.

With the Dodgers and Mets, Mike Piazza hit at least 30 homers in 10 out of 11 seasons, missing the mark only during the strike-shortened 1994 season. In 2004, he passed Carlton Fisk as the most prolific home run hitter among catchers.

Many of today's best catchers combine the power of Roy Campanella with the athleticism of Buck Ewing. Ivan "Pudge" Rodriguez is the only catcher to hit 25 homers and steal 35 bases in the same season, which he accomplished in 1999. That year he also won his ninth-consecutive Gold Glove award and became the first catcher to win an MVP award since Thurman Munson in 1976.

Mike Piazza, 1998

Ivan Rodriguez, 1998

THE FIRST BASEMAN

With a playing career that began when he was 19 years old and ended when he was 45, Adrian "Cap" Anson was the dominant first baseman of the nineteenth century. He batted over .300 in all but three of those 27 seasons. He led the league in runs batted in eight times and still ranks third on the all-time list. He had more extra-base hits than anybody prior to 1900. As a player-

Lou Gehrig, 1930s

Cap Anson tobacco card, 1887

manager, Anson led the White Stockings to five National League pennants between 1880 and 1886. He also was influential in establishing a ban against African Americans in organized professional baseball.

Lou Gehrig is widely considered the greatest first baseman ever. Although his career was cut short by a rare disease that now bears his name, Gehrig played more games at first base than all but two men since 1900. He won the Most Valuable Player award in 1927—the year his teammate Babe Ruth knocked 60 homers—by finishing in the top three in the league in every major statistical category, including batting average, RBI, runs, hits, doubles, triples, home runs, walks, slugging percentage, and on-base percentage. He won the Triple Crown in 1934 and captured his second MVP in 1936. Batting behind Ruth and later Joe DiMaggio—legendary run producers in their own right—in the Yankees lineup, Gehrig

Albert Pujols, 2006

drove in more than 150 runs a record seven times. He played on six championship teams with the Bronx Bombers and twice batted over .500 in the World Series. While his hitting numbers are impressive by any standard, the "Iron Horse" is probably best remembered for his consecutive-games record, which stood until Cal Ripken Jr. broke it in 1995, 56 years after Gehrig played his final game at the age of 35.

As a rookie, Albert Pujols split his time between first base, third base, and the outfield, and he didn't become St. Louis' regular first baseman until his fourth season. But his path to be-

coming one of the greatest ever to play the position seems clear. After winning the Rookie of the Year award in 2001 at the age of 21, Pujols went on to win the batting title in 2003 and the NL Most Valuable Player award in 2005. Pujols has batted over .300, hit more than 30 homers, and driven in at least 100 runs in each of his first six seasons. If he continues to hit home runs at the same pace that he has through his first five full seasons, Pujols will reach 700 career home runs by the time he's 38 years old—younger than Ruth, Aaron, and Bonds were when they reached that milestone.

The Second Baseman

Nobody has played more games at second base than Eddie Collins. Throughout his career, Collins got on base often (.424 career on-base percentage), stole a lot of bases (seventh on the all-time list), and was an expert bunter (first in career sacrifice hits). He was one of the best fielders at the position. Many who saw him play insist Collins was the greatest second baseman ever.

The one thing that Collins lacked in his game was power, but second basemen traditionally are not known for being home run hitters. Along with Collins, Rogers Hornsby and Joe Morgan are generally considered the best pivot men in history; both Hornsby and Morgan exhibited more power at the plate than Collins. Although Hornsby hit over 300 home runs in his career (not all coming while he was a second baseman), he is most remarkable for his batting average: his .358 lifetime mark is second only to Ty Cobb's. Over a five-year stretch from 1921 to 1925, Hornsby batted .402 with a .690 slugging percentage while knocking an average of 29 homers and driving in 120 runs per season. Morgan's 268 career dingers were, until 1996, the record for home runs hit while playing the position, but he never hit more than 27 in a season. A two-time MVP, Morgan's biggest strengths were his base stealing and fielding. Morgan won five-straight Gold Gloves with Cincinnati in the 1970s.

The record for consecutive Gold Glove awards by a second baseman belongs to Chicago's Ryne Sandberg, with nine. Sandberg is also the man who broke Morgan's record for home runs at the position. In 1990, he became the first second baseman since Hornsby to lead the league in homers. That same season, Sandberg completed a streak of 123 games without making an error, setting a new record previously held by Joe Morgan.

Defense will always be an essential quality for any second baseman. Jeff Kent hasn't won a Gold Glove in his first 14 seasons, but the five-time All-Star has passed Hornsby, Morgan, Sandberg, and every other second baseman on the career home run list. He also became the first second baseman to collect 100 or more RBI in six consecutive seasons.

Eddie Collins, 1927

Above: Ryne Sandberg, 1996

Facing page: Jeff Kent, 2006

THE SHORTSTOP

The stereotype of the all-glove, no-bat shortstop was shattered in the 1990s with an influx of multi-talented superstars at the position. A hundred years earlier, shortstop Honus Wagner was dominant in virtually every aspect of the game. He was the best fielder of his day, and one of the greatest ever. The "Flying Dutchman" also led the league in stolen bases five times, and his 252 career triples are the third most in history. On top of his eight batting crowns, Wagner posted the highest slugging percentage six times—only two other shortstops have led the league in slugging even once (Arky Vaughan in 1935 and Alex Rodriguez in 2003).

In a 19-year career, Ozzie Smith only once batted over .300 and his career slugging percentage was a paltry .328. Alex Rodriguez hit more home runs in his first full season (36) than Smith had in his entire career (28). Yet the "Wizard of Oz" was a first-ballot Hall of Famer and one of history's greatest shortstops. His 13-consecutive Gold Glove awards are unmatched at the position.

Smith is part of a long legacy of Gold-Glove-caliber shortstops who had relatively limited impact at the plate. Going back to the 1910s and 1920s, Hall of Famer Rabbit Maranville never batted above .300 in 17 full seasons. Luis Aparicio was among the best shortstops in the 1960s, and he earned a place in Cooperstown despite a career on-base percentage of just .311.

The emergence of Cal Ripken Jr. and Barry Larkin in the 1980s forever altered the perception of the position. Ripken won back-to-back Gold Gloves in 1991 and 1992, but he also won eight Silver Slugger awards (given annually to the top offensive player at each position). He broke Ernie Banks' career record for home runs as a shortstop. In his MVP season of 1991, Ripken batted .323 and slugged .566. Larkin, a three-time Gold Glove winner, was a nine-time Silver Slugger in the National League.

Between 1994 and 1997, four shortstops debuted in the American League who elevated the position to a new level. Derek Jeter batted over .300 in seven of his first ten seasons. Boston's

Ozzie Smith, 1985 World Series

Honus Wagner, 1911

Cal Ripken Jr., 1995

Nomar Garciaparra hit 65 homers in his first two full seasons and led the league in batting in 1999 and 2000. Miguel Tejada averaged 31 homers between 2000 and 2004 and drove in over 100 runs in each of those seasons. Alex Rodriguez established himself as one of the game's best as soon as he entered the league as an 18-year-old in 1994. He averaged 42.5 homers in his first eight seasons, including back-to-back 50-homer seasons in 2001 and 2002—a first among shortstops. Rodriguez had 400 career homers before he was 30 years old, making him the youngest to reach that milestone. Much more than a one-dimensional player, A-Rod won consecutive Gold Gloves in 2002 and 2003. He further showed his versatility by moving to third base after arriving in New York to play alongside Jeter in 2004.

Alex Rodriguez and Derek Jeter, 2000

THE DOUBLE PLAY

Chicago's Joe Tinker at short, Johnny Evers at second, and Frank Chance at first weren't the greatest double-play combination in history, but they are the most well-known. Immortalized in a verse by New York sportswriter Franklin P. Adams in 1910—"These are the saddest of possible words: 'Tinker to Evers to Chance' / Trio of bear cubs, and fleeter than birds, Tinker and Evers and Chance."—the trio were Cubs teammates for 11 seasons, including four pennant-winners between 1906 and 1910. All three infielders were elected to the Hall of Fame in the same year, 1946.

The other Chicago ballclub, the White Sox, had their own Hall of Fame double-play combo in the late 1950s and early 1960s. Shortstop Luis Aparicio, who had two stints with the Sox in his 18-

Luis Aparicio and Nellie Fox, Chicago White Sox, late 1950s

year career, trails only Ozzie Smith and Cal Ripken Jr. for double plays by a shortstop. Nellie Fox is second on the all-time list among second basemen. In 1959 and again in 1960, Fox and Aparicio both won the Gold Glove award for their respective positions. (There was no award in 1956, their first year as teammates, and in 1957 one award was given for both leagues.)

No middle infielder was involved in more double plays than Pittsburgh's Bill Mazeroski, the greatest-fielding second baseman of all-time. With Gold Glover Gene Alley at shortstop, the Pirates set a National League record with 215 double plays in 1966. Although Maz helped the Pirates turn seven double plays during the 1960 World Series against the Yankees, he is best remembered for his dramatic game-winning home run in the final game.

The period from 2001 to 2005 saw more double plays turned in the National League than any five-year span since Mazeroski's rookie season of 1956. Since 2001, no middle infielder has turned more double plays than Pittsburgh shortstop Jack Wilson. He and second baseman Jose Castillo helped the Pirates convert 194 double plays in 2005.

Joe Tinker, Johnny Evers, and Frank Chance, 1910

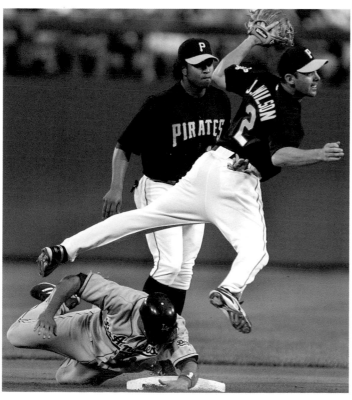

Above: Bill Mazeroski, 1960 World Series

Left: Jack Wilson, 2005

Brooks Robinson, 1975

THE THIRD BASEMAN

Known as the "hot corner," third base requires catlike reflexes to field the sharp liners that come screaming down the line. Traditionally it is also a position where teams hope to find home-run power at the plate. One of the first third basemen to display both sets of skills was Frank "Home Run" Baker. Although his tally of 96 career homers may belie his nickname, Baker led the league four years in a row during the dead-ball era. He earned the moniker during the 1911 World Series when he hit two clutch drives against the New York Giants. One of the greatest postseason performers in history, Baker batted .378 and drove in 18 runs in 20 games during four World Series with the Philadelphia Athletics.

Baker's home run total pales in comparison to the long-ball prowess of third basemen Eddie Mathews and Mike Schmidt, both of whom knocked over 500 in their careers. Schmidt led the league eight times, and he also won 10 Gold Glove awards. Brooks Robinson didn't hit half as many home runs as Schmidt did (though Robinson's 268 homers are respectable), but he had

as big an impact on the game as any third baseman. The 16-consecutive Gold Gloves by the "Human Vacuum Cleaner" is unprecedented for any position. Like Baker, Robinson was a force in the postseason as well. In 1970, he won the World Series MVP by batting .429 at the plate and smothering virtually everything that the Cincinnati Reds sent his way in the field.

The lead for Gold Glove awards among active third baseman lies with Scott Rolen, who is still 10 shy of Robinson. Before an injury-plagued season in 2005, Rolen had averaged 28 homers in his first eight seasons with the Phillies and Cardinals.

Atlanta's Chipper Jones has been one of the game's best run producers for a decade, and an integral piece in his team's 11-consecutive division titles since 1995, Jones' rookie season. He collected more than 100 RBI in six-straight years as a third baseman, and the switch-hitter averaged 31 homers in his first nine seasons. Although Jones' struggles with the glove led Braves manager Bobby Cox to move him to left field in 2002 and 2003, Jones has been back at the hot corner since 2004.

Above: Chipper Jones, 1996 World Series

Left: Frank "Home Run" Baker, circa 1910

Tris Speaker, 1918

THE OUTFIELDER

In 1910, the Boston Red Sox fielded a trio of 22-year-olds that would become the top outfield in the game for the next six seasons: Duffy Lewis in left, Tris Speaker in center, and Harry Hooper in right. Speaker, who was traded to Cleveland in 1916, was legendary for his range in the outfield. He preferred to play a very shallow center field, and in 1918 he turned two unassisted double plays at second base. To this day, Speaker holds the record for most assists by an outfielder. More than just a wizard with the glove, Speaker's .344 lifetime batting average is the sixth-best of all time. His quick reflexes and ability to anticipate where the ball was headed allowed him to chase down balls that most fielders would give up on.

Another all-time legend who rarely gave up on a fly ball was Willie Mays. Indeed, Mays caught more fly balls than any

Andruw Jones, 2004

outfielder in history. Mays was also arguably the greatest all-around talent ever to play baseball, possessing a rare combination of power, speed, and phenomenal fielding ability. In 1957, the Rawlings Sporting Goods Company introduced the Gold Glove award to honor the best fielders at each position. Mays won the award every year from its inception through 1968. He also led the league in homers four times and stolen bases four other times. Mays is the only player ever to amass 3,000 hits, 500 home runs, and 300 stolen bases in a career.

Willie Mays' greatness as a five-tool player (able to hit for average, hit for power, run, field, and throw) is unparalleled, but a handful of modern players have shown signs of Mays-like talent. Ken Griffey Jr. seemed well on his way—398 career homers, more than 1,100 RBI and 1,000 runs, 10 Gold Gloves, and 10-consecutive All-Star selections by the time he was 30—before injuries slowed his pace.

Today, Andruw Jones of Atlanta has a range in the field that is reminiscent of Mays. He has also averaged 33 homers through his first nine seasons, including a league-high 51 in 2005. Jones has batted over .300 only once, however, while striking out 100 or more times in each season.

Willie Mays at spring training, 1956

The ability to chase down fly balls is just one of the vital skills that a Gold Glove–caliber outfielder must possess. A strong arm to throw out daring runners is also important, particularly for those stationed out in right field. Center fielder Tris Speaker was one who possessed both skills. He threw out more runners on the base paths than any outfielder in history.

Roberto Clemente, the Puerto Rican–born outfielder who spent his entire career in Pittsburgh, had what many regard as the best outfield arm ever. He had more assists in the outfield than any player in modern baseball. One story has "the Great One" throwing a ball from deepest right-center field at Forbes Field all the way to home plate on a fly—nearly 460 feet away. With his all-around fielding skill, Clemente equaled Willie Mays' streak of 12-consecutive Gold Gloves before a plane crash in December 1972 ended his life and career at the age of 38.

In the outfield, Roberto Clemente's arm is most closely invoked today by that of Vladimir Guerrero. Guerrero's .324 average and 305 home runs in his first 10 seasons show Guerrero's strengths at the plate. He became the fifth player in history to collect at least 30 homers, 100 runs, 100 RBI, and a .300 average in each of his first five full major league seasons. His weaknesses with the leather have denied him Gold Glove honors, but his throwing arm is one of the best in the game.

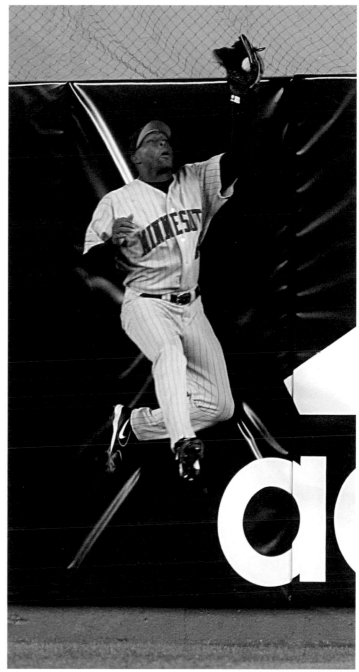

Torii Hunter, 2003

Torii Hunter has won five-straight Gold Gloves through 2005. Few outfielders in recent memory can match Hunter's athleticism in the field and his knack for snagging home runs balls headed over the fences.

Above: Vladimir Guerrero, 2006

Facing page: Roberto Clemente, 1958

Cy Young pitching at Huntington Avenue Grounds, circa 1903

THE STARTING PITCHER

The role of the starting pitcher has changed more dramatically than any other aspect of the game over the last 150 years—more than the proliferation of the home run, the demise of the stolen base and sacrifice bunt, the advent of the designated hitter, or anything else. Until the 1880s it was typical for a team to use only one pitcher over the course of an entire season. Throughout the nineteenth and into the early-twentieth century, it was simply assumed that the pitcher who started the game would finish it, unless things got really out of hand.

Charley "Old Hoss" Radbourn of the Providence Grays started 68 games in 1883 and completed 66 of them. He threw more than 632 innings and won 48 games. Old Hoss outdid himself the next year. He completed all 73 games that he started in 1884, won 59 of them, and pitched 678 innings. The last pitcher to throw as many as 300 innings in a season was Steve Carlton in 1980.

John Clarkson was another workhorse from the 1880s. In one five-year span with the Chicago White Stockings and Boston Red Stockings, Clarkson completed 295 of the 310 games he started, notched 2,716 innings pitched, and won 209 games between 1885 and 1889. By way of comparison, Pedro Martinez, who is considered a premier pitcher of the modern era, has pitched 2,513 innings, completed 46 games, and posted 197 wins in 13 seasons.

When Curt Schilling, another of today's finest hurlers, started the seventh game of the 2001 World Series for Arizona on "only" three days' rest, it was one of the year's biggest baseball stories. Randy Johnson pitching the final inning-and-a-third of that same game after going seven innings the night before was proclaimed as sheer heroism. Ninety-eight years earlier, Joe "Iron Man" McGinnity of the New York Giants started and won both games

Joe McGinnity, 1903

of a doubleheader—three times in the same month! McGinnity, whose nickname was a reflection of his offseason work at a foundry rather than his endurance on the mound, completed 82 percent of the games he started in his 10-year major league career.

The first pitch at Arizona's Bank One Ballpark, 1998

Pedro Martinez relieved by manager Terry Francona, 2004

The name Cy Young is synonymous with pitching supremacy. Other than Walter Johnson's 417 wins, nobody has come within 138 of Young's 511 career victories. Another record that is equally untouchable is Young's total of 749 complete games. To give that some perspective, Young completed more games than Roger Clemens, Greg Maddux, Randy Johnson, Curt Schilling, Mike Mussina, Tom Glavine, David Wells, John Smoltz, Pedro Martinez, and Brad Radke *combined*. The active leader, Clemens, has 118 complete games in 22 seasons—the same number of seasons that Young pitched.

THE RIGHT-HANDED ACE

New York's John McGraw built the foundation of a dynasty in the early 1900s on the arms of two right-handed pitchers: Christy Mathewson and Joe McGinnity. They each had back-to-back 30-win seasons in 1903 and 1904. McGinnity won only 21 to Matty's 31 in 1905, but the Giants won their first World Championship that year. Although McGinnity was out of the majors by 1909,

Mathewson was the game's dominant pitcher for more than a decade. Between 1903 and 1914, he was among the five-winningest National League pitchers in every single season.

The only time that Mathewson faced off against the American League's dominating right-hander of that era was for a charity game in 1911. Walter Johnson's Washington Senators never had the success that Mathewson's Giants had—the Senators didn't win

Christy Mathewson and Walter Johnson, 1911

2,000 K's. Ryan had only two seasons with 20 or more wins, but his seven no-hitters are testament to the power of his fastball. His last two no-hitters came in 1990 and 1991, when he was 43 and 44 years old.

By the time that Ryan retired in 1993 at the age of 46, another flamethrower had assumed the title of most fearsome righty. Roger Clemens had already won his third Cy Young award—three more than Ryan won in his 27 seasons—and four more were still to come for the Rocket. As Clemens winds down his Hall of Fame career in 2006, he will walk away from the game as the active leader in wins, strikeouts, innings pitched, complete games, and shutouts.

Nolan Ryan, 1990

a pennant until 1924—but that didn't affect Johnson's performance on the mound. As Washington's ace for two decades, Johnson led the American League in strikeouts 12 times, and he never finished out of the top five in 18 full seasons. His 3,508 career strikeouts stood as the record for more than 50 years. Johnson still holds the record for shutouts in a career (110). He also led the AL in wins six times and won the pitching triple crown (leading in wins, ERA, and strikeouts) three times.

Johnson pitched before the days of radar guns, but the "Big Train" had one of the most awesome fastballs in the history of baseball. Nolan Ryan also overpowered the opposition with his velocity, and he shattered Johnson's strikeout mark by more than

Roger Clemens, 2002

Eddie Plank, 1913

THE LEFT-HANDED ACE

Left-handed pitchers were a rarity in the nineteenth century. Before Eddie Plank, who was the first lefty to win 300 games, no southpaw had as many 200 wins in a career. Ed "Cannonball" Morris posted a record of 171 wins and 122 losses in the American Association, National League, and Players League from 1884 to 1890, but he was out of baseball by the age of 28.

Two hundred and eighty-four of Plank's 326 career wins came while pitching for Connie Mack's Philadelphia Athletics between 1901 and 1914. From 1902 to 1907, Plank was joined in the rotation by another Hall of Fame southpaw, Rube Waddell. The eccentric Waddell won at least 20 games four years in a row for the A's, and his 349 strikeouts in 1904 stood as the post-1900 record until

another southpaw, Sandy Koufax, topped it 61 years later. Lefties Plank and Waddell combined to win 267 games in six seasons as teammates.

Connie Mack must have had an affinity for lefties. The second left-handed pitcher to collect 300 wins was Lefty Grove, who won 195 of those games while pitching for the Athletics between 1925 and 1933. Mack paired Grove with another left-handed Rube—Rube Walberg, who won 130 games over the same nine-year span that Grove was in Philadelphia.

The winningest lefty in baseball history, Warren Spahn, was also part of a dangerous pitching duo, but Spahn's partner in crime, Johnny Sain, pitched with the other arm. In 1948, the lefty-righty tandem helped lead the Boston Braves to their first pennant in 34 years—and the saying "Spahn and Sain and pray for rain" among Braves fans was a reflection (perhaps unfair) of the limitations of the other pitchers on the staff. Spahn notched 20 wins in a season a record 13 times before he retired at the age of 44. He matched his career high of 23 wins when he was 42 years old—the oldest ever to reach that total. He also led the league in complete games seven consecutive times after his 36th birthday.

Following Spahn's long reign, Sandy Koufax and Randy Johnson have been the game's southpaw kings. Both struggled with control problems early in their careers, but while Koufax had to retire at the age of 30 due to chronic arthritis, Johnson has continued strong into his forties. He hurled a perfect game in May 2004 and became the oldest pitcher to accomplish the feat. Standing 6 feet 10 inches tall and possessing a fastball that can top 100 miles per hour, Randy Johnson is one of the most intimidating presences to ever take the mound. The fact that he has hit more batters with pitches than any other active pitcher only reinforces that aura of intimidation.

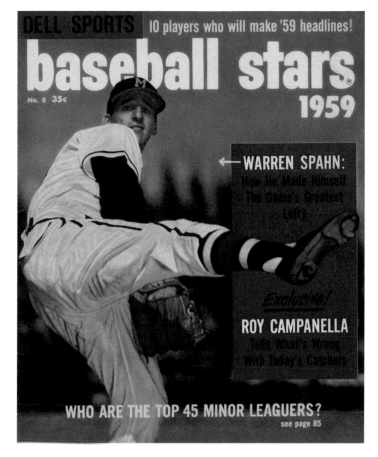

Right: Warren Spahn, 1959

Below. Randy Johnson, 2002

THE PITCHING MOTION

Nineteenth-century hurlers didn't have the advantage of throwing from a mound, and before 1884 they weren't even allowed to pitch overhand. Until the 1870s the pitcher was prohibited from bending his elbow or wrist. For a time the pitcher had to keep both feet on the ground, and from 1879 to 1884 he couldn't turn his back to the batter. The rules at one point allowed the batter to instruct the pitcher where he wanted the pitch located.

Once the restrictions on the pitching motion were erased from the rule book, pitchers employed a variety of delivery styles to try

Byung-Hyun Kim, 2005

Carl Mays, circa 1920

Sketch of pitcher in pitcher's box, 1875

to keep batters off guard. Carl "Sub" Mays was a star in the 1910s and 1920s with his sidearm or underarm delivery. Mays' deceptive delivery had tragic consequences, however, in August of 1920 when he beaned Cleveland's Ray Chapman with a pitch. Chapman died within hours.

Relievers Kent Tekulve and Dan Quisenberry brought the submarine pitch back into prominence in the 1970s and 1980s. Byung-Hyun Kim's quirky motion helped the Arizona Diamondbacks reach the World Series in 2001—even if the Yankees were able to solve the mystery of his delivery during the series, to the tune of

Orlando Hernandez, 1999

Juan Marichal, 1960s

six hits and five runs in less than four innings. With the Colorado Rockies in 2005 and 2006, Kim became a part-time starter.

The high leg kick is another technique pitchers have used to try to disorient the hitter. The most famous progenitor of the high-kick delivery was Juan Marichal in the 1960s. Orlando "El Duque" Hernandez brought his own style of unorthodox leg kick to the major leagues after defecting from Cuba in 1998.

SPITBALLS AND SCUFFING

Before 1920, pitchers made little effort to disguise their attempts at doctoring the ball. There were no rules to prohibit the throwing of spitballs, grease balls, mud balls, scuff balls, or otherwise-defaced baseballs. In fact, several pitchers in the early-twentieth century built careers on such trick pitches. When the league banned spitballs and its variations in 1920 (in the wake of the fatal beaning of Ray Chapman by a Carl Mays spitter), the 17 pitchers who were known spitballers at the time were allowed to continue using the trick pitches. Foremost among them was Burleigh Grimes, then a 26-year-old righty with the Brooklyn Dodgers. Grimes chewed slippery elm to help activate his salivary glands. The future Hall of Famer pitched for 14 more seasons after the ban, and he won 20 or more games five times during the 1920s.

When Grimes retired in 1934, he was the last of the legal spitballers, but he was hardly the last pitcher to doctor a baseball. Several modern-day pitchers have been associated with foreign substances and other forms of doctoring. Gaylord Perry was the most notorious, and successful, spitballer of the modern era. His 1974 autobiography was entitled, *Me and the Spitter*. The Hall of Famer won 314 games and struck out more than 3,500 batters in his 22-year career. Despite his reputation for throwing Vaseline-covered baseballs, Perry was not ejected from a game for throwing an illegal pitch until 1983, his 20th season in the majors.

In 1987, Minnesota Twins pitcher Joe Niekro was searched on the mound during a game against the California Angels under suspicion of doctoring the ball. After checking his glove, the umpires asked him to empty his pockets. Niekro reached into his back pocket and nonchalantly tossed an object out of the umpire's line of sight. His maneuver did not go unnoticed. The umpire

Burleigh Grimes, 1932

picked up the emery board and immediately ejected Niekro. The knuckleballer's explanation was that he had been filing his fingernails between innings and forgot to put away the emery board. He received a 10-game suspension.

Left: Gaylord Perry, 1979

Below: Joe Niekro, caught in the act, 1987

The Reliever

The idea of giving a pitcher the specific job of finishing games was unheard of before 1900. The first pitcher with at least 25 appearances in a season who relieved more games than he started was Clark Griffith in 1905. In the waning years of a successful career as a starter, Griffith pitched in 42 games for the New York Highlanders (Yankees) in 1905 and 1906 and appeared in relief in all but nine of them. The tactician who employed this innovative strategy was none other than Griffith himself, serving as player-manager.

John McGraw used the erratic Doc Crandall in a similar mop-up role a few years later. Crandall appeared in 185 games for the Giants from 1909 to 1913 but started only 53. By the 1920s, dedicated relievers were employed more frequently around the league. In 1925, Firpo Marberry pitched in 55 games for the Washington

Senators, and didn't start a single one. The following season he became the first pitcher to save as many as 20 games in a season, and his 22 saves stood as the record until 1948. (The save did not become an official statistic until 1969.) In 10 seasons with Washington, Marberry appeared in 332 games in relief.

Even as the role of relievers became more established in the 1920s, starting pitchers still completed nearly half of all games. By the 1950s, the league-wide complete-game rate had dropped to about a third, and relievers were being given more specialized roles—long relief, set-up men, and closers—rather than just coming in to bail out a struggling starter.

The heyday of the reliever arrived in the 1970s and 1980s. Rollie Fingers, Mike Marshall, Sparky Lyle, Goose Gossage, Bruce Sutter, Kent Tekulve, and Dan Quisenberry all played key roles in leading teams to the World Series. Fingers was the ace reliever on three World Champion teams in Oakland and one in Milwaukee. He also led the NL in saves two years running as a closer for the San Diego Padres.

Today, starters complete less than five percent of the games. Bullpens are filled with pitchers who have narrowly-defined roles. One reliever might be called upon only to face a left-handed batter in a certain situation, while another will be brought in only if a right-handed hitter is due up. Most ace closers are expected to pitch no more than an inning at a time, and usually only if the team has a close lead. The strategy of the highly structured bullpen was pioneered by manager Tony Larussa and used to great effect with closer Dennis Eckersley in Oakland.

During the Yankees' run of five pennants from 1998 to 2003, the team's most valuable player was Mariano Rivera. He saved 35 or more games eight times in nine seasons, including two years with at least 50. Relying on basically two pitches—the fastball and the cut fastball—he has posted a career ERA of 2.04 since taking over the closer role in 1997. His postseason performances have been even more remarkable: 34 saves, 17 wins, and a 0.81 ERA in 72 games. Rivera won the World Series MVP in 1999 and the ALCS MVP in 2003. To illustrate the narrowing role of the closer, Rivera has averaged about an inning per appearance since 1997.

Firpo Marberry, 1928

Rollie Fingers, 1974 All-Star Game

Mariano Rivera, 2004 American League Championship Series

THE MANAGER

When Connie Mack retired as manager of the Philadelphia Athletics in 1950, the team had to hire a new skipper for the first time in its history. Mack managed the team in its inaugural season of 1901 and left 7,466 games later. (Mack also owned part of the team since 1901 and became sole owner in 1936.) In the 55 years since Mack retired, the A's have had 27 different managers. Mack's replacement, Jimmie Dykes, lasted just three seasons.

No baseball owner today has a bigger reputation for having a short fuse with his managers than the Yankees' George Steinbrenner. Indeed, he hired and fired Billy Martin on five different occasions between 1975 and 1988. Since Steinbrenner took the reins in New York in 1973, the Yankees have had 15 different men serve as manager. The Chicago Cubs, meanwhile, have

Connie Mack and John McGraw, 1911 World Series

had 21 different managers over the same period. The teams that have had the greatest managerial stability are the Los Angeles Dodgers and Minnesota Twins, each of whom has had just seven skippers since 1973.

With 50 years of service to the same team, Connie Mack outlasted the next-longest-tenured manager of any team by two decades. John McGraw, who faced Mack three times in the World Series, led the New York Giants for 31 seasons. In 2006, Bobby Cox entered his 21st year with the Atlanta Braves, including a four-year stint from 1978 to 1981. Since retaking the helm in 1990, Cox has piloted the Braves to 14 division titles in 15 seasons. Joe Torre has lasted more than a decade under Steinbrenner in New York, and his four World Series victories (two of them over Cox's Braves) are tops among active managers.

Before managing the A's, Connie Mack was a player-manager for three seasons in Pittsburgh, serving as a part-time back-up catcher and first baseman. Charles Comiskey played first base for the Browns and Reds in all 12 seasons that he managed the teams. Cap Anson worked for 20 seasons as both manager and first baseman, and won five National League pennants in the process. A dozen Hall of Fame players directed teams to World Championships while also managing the team, including Tris

Pete Rose, 1985

Speaker (1920 Indians), Rogers Hornsby (1926 Cardinals), and Frank Chance (1907 and 1908 Cubs).

The player-manager is extinct in baseball today. About 250 men in the history of the game have played the dual role at some point during their careers, if even for just a few games. Since 1950, there have been 12 player-managers, and most of those saw limited action as they went through the motions of their final season or two as active players. Pete Rose was the last active player to also manage, leading the Reds to a 194-170 record while appearing in 194 games at first base from 1984 to 1986.

Bobby Cox and Joe Torre, 1997 All-Star Game

Monte Irvin stealing home, 1951 World Series

STRATEGIES OF THE GAME

The value of plays such as the sacrifice bunt and the stolen base faces much scrutiny these days. With only 27 outs to spare over the course of a nine-inning game, the argument goes, why *give* one away with a sacrifice bunt just to advance the runner a single base? Indeed, in an era when home runs are so prevalent and one swing of the bat can advance a runner all the way around the bases, driving the ball over the fence seems a more efficient strategy than bunting the ball along the infield grass.

Back in the dead-ball era, when over-the-fence homers were not so easy to come by, teams employed so-called small-ball to pro-

duce runs. Also known as "inside baseball," the strategy looked to the hit-and-run, drag bunts, Baltimore chops, and the double steal to gain any extra base. The Boston Red Stockings are credited with developing the hit-and-run in the 1880s. The Baltimore Orioles are famous for perfecting it in the 1890s. Baltimore's top hitter, Willie Keeler, was expert at hitting the ball to the spot vacated by the fielder going to make a play on the advancing base runner. Keeler was also one of the game's great bunters; he ranks fourth all-time in sacrifice hits.

The power surge that arrived in the 1920s shifted the focus from manufacturing runs one base at a time to capitalizing on the newfound potential of the long ball. In 1917, major leaguers knocked 335 home runs and executed 3,079 sacrifices. The disparity narrowed after 1920, and by 1937, the number of home runs surpassed the number of sacrifice hits for the first time. By the year 2000, home runs outnumbered sacrifices by more than three to one. When Ray Chapman set the single-season record of 67 sacrifice hits in 1917, the American League leader in home runs was Wally Pipp with 12. When Barry Bonds set the single-season record of 73 homers in 2001, David Eckstein led the AL with 16 sacrifices.

Although stolen bases had a resurgence during the 1970s and 1980s on the heels of Lou Brock and Rickey Henderson, the stolen base has gone through a similar decline since the dead-ball days.

In every season from 1901 through 1918, the league-wide average was at least one stolen base per game. By the end of the 1920s, the number of stolen bases had dropped to less than half its pre-1920 average.

The integration of Major League Baseball in 1947 brought in many talented players from the Negro Leagues with aggressive base-running skills, including Jackie Robinson and Monte Irvin. In just 10 seasons in the majors, Robinson stole home plate 19 times, the most in modern history. Irvin stole home five times during the 1951 season alone, and he did it again in the first inning of the first game of that year's World Series against the Yankees. Despite such daring speedsters, the 12 lowest years for stolen bases in baseball history were 1947 to 1959.

Willie Keeler bunting, 1906

Willy Taveras bunting, 2006

Mike Cameron attempting to steal home, 2001

THE UMPIRE

Baseball's on-field arbiters of the rules are both a symbol of authority and a target of abuse. In the formative years of the sport, the lone umpire for a game was selected by the home team, with approval by the visitors, from among the bystanders or even from among the players. The umpire was treated as an honored authority.

In 1878, the National League ruled that umpires should be paid five dollars by the home team. A year later it established a regular staff of 20 from which the teams could select an umpire, who generally lived in the city where the game was played. The tendency toward hometown bias encouraged the league to hire a salaried staff of traveling umpires in 1883, as the American Association had done the year before.

Beginning in 1879, the umpires were authorized to impose fines on players for breaking the rules and even for foul language. This did not stop the threats and intimidation, however. The 1890s was a notoriously rough time in baseball, with violence real or threatened from both players and fans, and umpires frequently required police escorts when exiting the ballpark. Ban Johnson, president of the American League from 1901 to 1927, was a major force in

Bill Klem, 1940

restoring respect and honor to the umpiring profession.

In the nineteenth century one umpire worked each game, and in the early days he sat far back from the plate or along the foul line. Once umpires adopted the masks and chest protectors that catchers used, they moved directly behind the plate. Two umps per game were standard in both the American and National Leagues by 1912: one stationed behind the plate and another in the field.

World Series games were officiated by four umpires from 1909 until 1947. The crew at the 1916 series included future Hall of Famer Tommy Connelly as well as Hank O'Day. Connelly and O'Day formed the umpiring duo for the first World Series in 1903. Bill Dinneen, who pitched for Boston in the 1903 series, is the only man to play and umpire in the Fall Classic. Nobody umpired in more World Series (18) than Hall of Famer Bill Klem. The World Series went to six umpires in 1947, and the four-person crew has been used in all regular-season games since 1950.

Nineteenth-century umpire pelted with debris, from America's National Game

The power to fine players and managers for illegal actions passed from umpires to the league presidents in the 1950s, but umpires still can eject unruly participants from a game. Some managers made arguing with the umpire an art form, most notably Casey Stengel, Leo Durocher, Earl Weaver, Billy Martin, and Lou Piniella. Some umps take equal pleasure in jawing back at the uppity players and managers.

Left: Umpires Chuck Meriweather, Ted Barrett, Jim Evans, and Larry McCoy, 1999

Below: Umpires Ernie Quigley, Tommy Connelly, Hank O'Day, and Bill Dinneen, 1916 World Series

Commissioner Landis and members of the 1919 Chicago White Sox, 1920

SCANDALS

Gambling was a popular activity among fans at ballgames from about the time of the sport's inception. A few ballparks even set aside dedicated gambling sections in the grandstand. Gambling involving the players, however, has always been seen as a scourge on the game.

Even after baseball turned professional in the 1870s, many players were willing to throw a game in exchange for the extra cash. In 1877, five players from the Louisville Grays were banned from baseball for accepting money from gamblers. The first prominent player in the twentieth century to be implicated in fixing games was Hal Chase, a first baseman with the New York Highlanders

and Cincinnati Reds. On several occasions he was suspected of taking bribes from gamblers, and he was suspended by Reds manager Christy Mathewson in 1918.

Gambling in baseball came under the national spotlight when eight players from the Chicago White Sox conspired to fix the outcome of the 1919 World Series. First baseman Chick Gandil and shortstop Swede Risberg were the ringleaders of the operation in cahoots with mobster Arnold Rothstein. In addition to Gandil and Risberg, the other conspirators were pitchers Eddie Cicotte and Lefty Williams; infielders Buck Weaver and Fred McMullin; and outfielders Happy Felsch and Joe Jackson. Judge Kenesaw

Mountain Landis was brought in to serve as league commissioner shortly after the scandal, and although the players were acquitted in court, Landis banned all eight from professional baseball for life. The accomplishments of Joe Jackson, one of the greatest hitters of all-time, remain forever clouded by his involvement in the Black Sox Scandal. Landis dedicated the next two decades of his term as commissioner to restoring integrity to the game.

A similar blow to baseball's integrity emerged in the 1990s. The rapid increase in the number of home runs during the decade raised suspicions that players were using performance-enhancing drugs. While Mark McGwire, Sammy Sosa, and Barry Bonds laid waste to the old home run records, ex-players like Ken Caminiti and Jose Canseco admitted to having used steroids as players, and both claimed that "juicing" was rampant among major leaguers.

The scandal led the United States Congress to hold hearings in March of 2005 to review Major League Baseball's drug policy. Among those called to testify were McGwire, Sosa, Rafael Palmeiro, and pitcher Curt Schilling, in addition to commissioner Bud Selig and other league executives. Bonds was involved in a

Barry Bonds, 2006

Steroid hearings, 2005

separate federal investigation into steroid distribution by Bonds' personal trainer and the Bay Area Laboratory Co-Operative (BALCO). The book *Game of Shadows* in 2006 further asserted that Bonds had been using the illegal substances for years. Some critics contend that all of Bonds' accomplishments since 1998 should be completely discredited.

From gambling to labor strikes to steroids, baseball has had its share of scandals, but it always manages to bounce back and recapture fans' attention once the dust settles.

THE COMMISSIONER

The dominant figure in the National League following its formation in 1876 was William Hulbert. He was the league's chief founder, and he served as its president from 1877 until his death in 1882. Hulbert fought to uphold the power of the team owners, and railed against the activities that had contributed to the demise of the NL's predecessor, the player-controlled National Association: gambling, "revolving" (players switching teams at will during the season in search of better pay), and teams failing to complete their schedules. He expelled the Philadelphia and New York teams from the league after the first season for the latter offense, and he banned four Louisville players in 1877 for fixing games.

After the American League established itself as a worthy peer to the National League at the turn of the twentieth century, the two leagues got together and formed a National Commission to serve as the controlling body for organized baseball. The commis-

Kenesaw Mountain Landis, 1920s

National Commission, 1909

sion was composed of the presidents of each league and a chairman selected by the presidents. Garry Herrmann, owner of the Cincinnati Reds, was appointed chairman, but the commission was dominated by American League president Byron Bancroft "Ban" Johnson from its inception.

The scandal of the 1919 World Series pushed baseball owners to abolish the already-weakening National Commission and replace it with a single individual with no direct connections to any team. The new position would have full, independent authority and be the final arbiter in all disputes involving leagues, teams, or players. The man selected for the role was federal judge Kenesaw Mountain Landis. Landis was unanimously elected by the owners as baseball's first commissioner in November 1920. He held the post until his death in 1944. Landis' most famous legacy was expelling the eight players involved in the Black Sox Scandal and helping to restore Americans' faith in the national pastime. Landis ruled with similarly firm authority for most of his time in office. In addition to the Chicago eight, he banned from the game no fewer than half a dozen players for fixing games or otherwise associating with gamblers.

Eight men have held the position of Commissioner of Baseball since Landis. Bowie K. Kuhn, elected in 1969, is the second-longest tenured. During his 15-year term, baseball abolished the reserve clause, introduced free agency, and had its first players' strike in 1981. It also saw a dramatic rise in attendance and the greatest period of league expansion.

Allan H. "Bud" Selig has served as Commissioner of Baseball since 1998, and he has been the central figure in administering Major League Baseball since his predecessor, Fay Vincent, resigned in 1992. Following Vincent's departure, an Executive Council of team owners ruled in the absence of a commissioner. Selig, who owned the Milwaukee Brewers, was the driving force behind the council until he was officially elected commissioner in July of 1998. Selig's tenure has seen significant changes in the game, such as the institution of interleague play, expansion of the postseason, and revenue sharing. But baseball has had its blemishes under Selig. The 272-day players' strike in 1994 was the longest work stoppage in baseball history, and the steroid scandal has plagued the league for nearly a decade with very slow response from the league office.

Bud Selig, 2005

Cincinnati Red Stockings, 1869

SALARIES

A columnist for the Boston *Globe,* writing about baseball's ever-rising salaries, commented on how the top ballplayers earn "as much money working a few hours each day during seven months as many college professors receive for their entire year's services." The article continues: "New York has the two men who are paid more for playing ball than any others in the world." No, not Alex Rodriguez and Derek Jeter. This writer is talking about New York Gothams Buck Ewing and John Montgomery Ward in 1884, who earned a combined $6,100 that year. (For the record, Jeter and A-Rod are estimated to take home a combined $46,280,727 in 2006.)

Ever since the Cincinnati Red Stockings became the first openly professional team in 1869, the matter of players' salaries has been a contentious issue. For most of baseball's first 100 years, the balance of power lay heavily in the owners' favor. The

Philadelphia's $100,000 infield, circa 1911

reserve clause, which served to lock up a player for as long as the owner wanted to keep him, first went into effect in 1879 and was gradually expanded during the 1880s. By 1887 virtually every professional ballplayer in the nation was covered by the reserve clause. John Ward was the most vocal opponent of the system, likening players under the reserve rule to sheep and chattel. In 1885, he helped to establish the Brotherhood of Professional Base Ball Players, the first players' union.

Ward's Brotherhood and several subsequent efforts to form unions failed to take hold, until the Major League Baseball Player's Association was formed in 1966. In the age of the reserve clause, a player's main bargaining chip was the holdout. Many prominent stars simply refused to play until the club's owner agreed to renegotiate the salary. Ty Cobb held out several times in his career, as did Cincinnati outfielder Edd Roush. Joe DiMaggio was soundly attacked by the media for holding out in 1938, after just his second season, and he ultimately relented. Pitchers Sandy Koufax and Don Drysdale held out in tandem in 1966 and were rewarded with contracts worth $125,000 and $110,000, respectively.

When Connie Mack assigned Stuffy McInnis to be the Philadelphia Athletics' first baseman in 1911 to play alongside Eddie Collins at second, Frank Baker at third, and Jack Barry at shortstop, the quartet was branded the "$100,000 Infield." That amount of money was quite exorbitant at the time—but the nickname was no reflection of the players' salaries, only their value to the team. Cobb was the game's best player in 1912, and he earned only $9,000.

The demise of the reserve clause in 1975 and the ensuing era of free agency—along with lucrative television contracts, sponsorship deals, and other revenue streams—has led to an explosion in salaries over the last 30 years. In 2005, the average salary among major leaguers was $2,476,589. The minimum salary in 2006 was $327,000. According to the Associated Press, at least 60 players earn more than $10 million a year (including bonuses and other guaranteed income). Rodriguez signed his 10-year, $250 million contract with the Texas Rangers in 2001. His 2006 share amounts to roughly $25,680,727.

New York's $25,000,000 infielder, 2004

THE OWNERS

In the first organized baseball league, the National Association, the team owners were little more than financial backers; the league was controlled by the players. William Hulbert made sure when he formed the National League in 1876 that owners would call the shots. Through the reserve clause and other practices, the owners maintained the upper hand during most of the game's history.

Many early owners held more than one position within the world of baseball. Alfred J. Reach of the Philadelphia Phillies and Albert G. Spalding of the Chicago White Stockings ran the two dominant sporting goods companies while also owning shares in their teams. Frank and Stanley Robison, proprietors of the Cleveland Spiders, purchased the St. Louis Brown Stockings in 1898 and transferred most of the Spiders' best players to St. Louis; the Spiders went 20-140 in 1899 and folded after the season. Barney Dreyfuss had a similar situation as owner of both the Louisville Colonels and the Pittsburgh Pirates. When the National League contracted from twelve teams to eight, the Colonels were one of the clubs on the chopping block, so Dreyfuss transferred the best Louisville players—including Honus Wagner—to Pittsburgh.

Charles Comiskey (seated, far left) with other American League owners, circa 1905

Former players were also prominent team owners in the first half of the twentieth century. Connie Mack was a (mediocre) catcher for the Washington Nationals and Pittsburgh Pirates before he made his way to the Philadelphia Athletics as manager and owner, where he remained for half a century. Clark Griffith won more than 230 games as a pitcher during his 20-year career, including three seasons as player-manager for the Washington Senators. He became the team's principal owner from 1920 to 1955. One of the finest first baseman of the 1880s was Charles Comiskey, and as player-manager of the St. Louis Browns he won four-consecutive American Association titles. In 31 years as owner of the Chicago White Sox, Comiskey was a notorious cheapskate, a quality that motivated eight of his players to accept money from gamblers to throw the 1919 World Series.

The most colorful owner of the mid-twentieth century was Bill Veeck. Among his legendary antics, Veeck hired the 3-foot-7-inch Eddie Gaedel as a pinch hitter for the St. Louis Browns in 1952; he held "Grandstand Managers Day" in St. Louis, at which he handed out placards to the fans to make strategy decisions during the course of a game; he installed the "Exploding Scoreboard" at Comiskey Park while owner of the Chicago White Sox; and he hosted "Disco Demolition Night" at Comiskey in 1979, which turned into a riot. Veeck also led the Cleveland Indians to a World Championship in 1948, and signed Larry Doby, the first African American player in the American League. In 1959, Veeck's White Sox won their first pennant since the Black Sox of 1919.

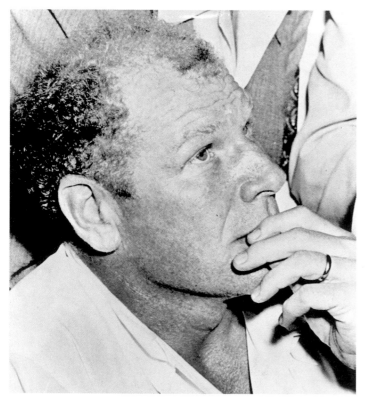

Bill Veeck

Ted Turner, 1976

In the 1970s, the arrival of free agency brought the wealthiest, and in some cases most eccentric, owners to the forefront. George Steinbrenner, who earned his riches in the Cleveland shipping industry, purchased the New York Yankees in 1973 and guided the team back to dynasty status within five years. He also constantly fought with his managers—most notably Billy Martin—recklessly spent millions on free agents, and associated with gamblers to try to discredit his star player, Dave Winfield, which led to Steinbrenner's suspension from baseball.

Ted Turner used his millions to buy the Atlanta Braves in 1976, and over the next two decades he helped to build one of the most dominant franchises in modern National League history. He was passionate about the team and popular among his players—although his one attempt at managing, taking over the team in the midst of an extended losing streak in 1977, left him with an 0-1 career managerial record. Turner's involvement in the team lessened after he merged with AOL-Time Warner in 1996, and he stepped down entirely in 2003.

George Steinbrenner with manger Billy Martin and general manager Lou Piniella, 1988

THE PRESS

The media has been covering baseball since its origins. Newspapers in the 1860s and 1870s printed recaps and box scores of games from all over the nation. Photographers attended games as soon as the camera was portable enough to carry onto the field, and they often positioned themselves in the midst of the action on the field of play. During the 1913 World Series at the Polo Grounds, several rows of reporters sat behind home plate with their telegraph machines ready to tap the events of the Giants-Athletics matchup to locations from coast to coast. Just eight years later, in August of 1921, KDKA in Pittsburgh broadcast the first major league game over the radio. The first televised game was in August 1939 at Ebbets Field, a contest between the Reds and Dodgers, with the legendary broadcaster Red Barber announcing. By the 1950s, baseball was being televised across the nation on a weekly basis.

Before television and radio allowed fans to experience the action as it was happening, it was the job of the journalist and sportswriter to re-create the drama and emotion of the moment. Henry Chadwick was one of the first and most influential writers to cover baseball. He helped to explain the young sport to a wide audience and conveyed the subtleties of the game. Esteemed sportswriters such as Ring Lardner, Damon Runyon, Grantland Rice, Red Smith, Heywood Broun, Shirley Povich, and others took up the art form in the twentieth century and helped to elevate the game's

Tris Speaker as a radio broadcaster, 1930s

heroes with their prose. The modern media of radio and television established their own legends, from Red Barber and Mel Allen to Vin Scully and Jack Buck. Ex-players brought a unique perspective while imparting the events of the game, and since the 1930s the broadcast booths have been graced with baseball legends, from Tris Speaker and Dizzy Dean to Joe Morgan and Tom Seaver. Tim McCarver played in the major leagues for two decades and has been covering baseball on television for even longer. He has covered more World Series than any broadcaster in history.

Both radio and television were initially viewed with much suspicion by baseball owners, who believed that people would stop coming to the ballpark if they could just stay at home and follow

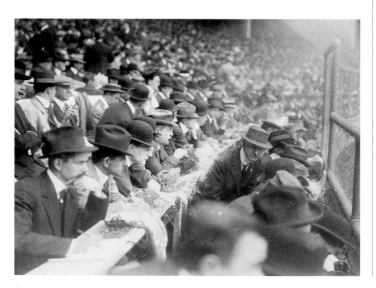

Press box at the Polo Grounds, 1913 World Series

the action. In the end, of course, the two media have helped to broaden the sport's popularity by bringing it into the living rooms of millions and millions of fans around the globe. The emergence of national cable networks—beginning with the Superstations of WTBS and WGN and exploding with the ESPN and FoxSports networks—now provide a regular diet of games and snapshot highlights of all the action on a nightly basis. Fans almost anywhere on the planet can follow the live progress of any game through web-casts on the internet. The number of people writing about baseball, from trained journalists to bloggers, has grown exponentially, leading to deeper and deeper analysis and investigation into our national game and its heroes and anti-heroes.

Television cameras in the Yankee Stadium press box, 1950

Below: Tim McCarver in the Yankee Stadium press box, 2003

Photographers catch Joe DiMaggio in action, 1938

Photographers at the Polo Grounds, 1910s

Mark McGwire surrounded by media, 1998

BIBLIOGRAPHY

Gershman, Michael. *Diamonds: The Evolution of the Ballpark.* New York: Houghton Mifflin, 1993.

James, Bill. *The New Bill James Historical Baseball Abstract.* Rev. ed. New York: The Free Press, 2001.

Johnson, Lloyd. *Baseball's Book of Firsts.* Philadelphia: Courage Books, 1999.

Leventhal, Josh. *Take Me Out to the Ballpark.* Rev. ed. New York: Black Dog & Leventhal, 2006.

Leventhal, Josh. *The World Series: An Illustrated History of the Fall Classic.* 4th ed. New York: Black Dog & Leventhal, 2005.

Nemec, David. *The Great Encyclopedia of 19th Century Major League Baseball.* New York: Donald I. Fine Books, 1997.

Palmer, Pete, and Gary Gillette. *The Baseball Encyclopedia.* New York: Barnes & Noble Books, 2004.

Rutledge Books. *A Baseball Century: The First 100 Years of the National League.* New York: Macmillan Publishing, 1976.

Seymour, Harold. *Baseball: The Golden Age.* New York, Oxford University Press, 1989.

Sullivan, Dean, ed. *Early Innings: A Documentary History of Baseball, 1825–1908.* Lincoln, Neb.: Bison Books, 1995.

Sullivan, Dean, ed. *Middle Innings: A Documentary History of Baseball, 1900–1948.* Lincoln, Neb.: Bison Books, 1998.

Thorn, John, Pete Palmer, and Michael Gershman, eds. *Total Baseball.* 7th ed. Kingston, NY: Total Sports Publishing, 2001.

Waggoner, Glen, Kathleen Moloney, and Hugh Howard. *Spitters, Bean-Balls, and the Incredible Shrinking Strike Zone.* Red. ed. Chicago: Triumph Books, 2000.

Ward, Geoffery C., and Ken Burns. *Baseball: An Illustrated History.* New York: Alfred A. Knopf, 1994.

INDEX